AR PTS: 4.0

CULTURES OF THE WORLD®

VIETNAM

Audrey Seah / Charissa M. Nair

BENCHMARK BOOKS

MARSHALL CAVENDISH
NEW YORK

PICTURE CREDITS
Cover photo: © Catherine Karnow/CORBIS
Richard l'Anson: 12, 56, 70, 81, 89, 122, 125, 126, 127 • APA: 8, 11, 36, 37, 39, 40, 52, 53,
54, 55, 58, 71, 75, 79, 83, 86, 88, 101, 115, 121, 123 • AsianFoodPix.com: 130 • Bes Stock:
9, 45, 112 • HBL Network: 6, 16, 19, 34, 49, 60, 74, 108, 110, 120 • Hulton Deutsch: 24,
26 • Hutchison Library: 17, 72, 80, 114, 119, 128 • Björn Klingwall: 10, 31, 35, 38, 41,
59, 61, 62, 64, 68, 85, 96, 109, 124 • Life File: 102 • Lonely Planet Images: 131 • Joseph
Lynch: 3, 4, 18, 22, 27, 29, 51, 57, 63, 65, 66, 67, 69, 73, 76, 78, 84, 90, 93, 94, 95, 97, 103,
105, 106, 107, 111, 113, 117, 118 • Gilles Massot: 20, 42, 92, 104 • Audrey Seah: 7, 21, 87
• David Simson: 1, 5, 28, 46, 50, 82 • Travel Ink: 44, 47, 48, 99 • Wilm Van Cappellen:
30 • Vietnamese Embassy, Singapore: 23, 32

ACKNOWLEDGMENTS
Thanks to Diane N. Fox of the Department of Anthropology at the University of
Washington for her expert reading of this manuscript

PRECEDING PAGE
A group of Vietnamese youth on an outing. Almost 30 percent of Vietnam's population
consists of people 14 years of age or younger.

Marshall Cavendish Benchmark
99 White Plains Road
Tarrytown, NY 10591
Website: www.marshallcavendish.us

© Times Media Private Limited 1996, 1994
© Marshall Cavendish International (Asia) Private Limited 2004
All rights reserved. First edition 1994. Second edition 2004.

® "Cultures of the World" is a registered trademark of Marshall Cavendish Corporation.

Originated and designed by Times Books International
An imprint of Marshall Cavendish International (Asia) Private Limited
A member of Times Publishing Limited

Library of Congress Cataloging-in-Publication Data
Seah, Audrey, 1958-
Vietnam / Audrey Seah.— 2nd ed.
    p. cm. — (Cultures of the world)
Includes bibliographical references and index.
    ISBN 0-7614-1789-3
1. Vietnam—Juvenile literature. I. Title. II. Series: Cultures of the world (2nd ed.)
DS556.3.S4 2004
959.704—dc22   2004012903

Printed in China

7 6 5 4 3 2

CONTENTS

A fruit seller perches on her table near a pile of ripe, red rambutans.

Some travel by boat down the numerous rivers of Vietnam, while others may prefer to ride a water buffalo.

INTRODUCTION

IN THE LAST TWO CENTURIES, Vietnam has experienced a series of dramatic changes: from a 2,000-year-old kingdom with an emperor and a ruling class of mandarins, to a French colony, to a divided country with two opposing philosophies of government, to reunification in 1975. Along the way, its people have experienced oppression, hardship, and poverty, but today Vietnam is a modern country filled with potential. The land is fertile and supports an agricultural economy based on the growing of rice and other crops. A wide variety of minerals are found in the mountains, and the seabed off the coast holds rich deposits of oil. Despite Vietnam's ongoing economic liberalization and the pressures of rapid development, this dignified country has managed to preserve its rich history and culture. This book, part of the *Cultures of the World* series, describes Vietnam, its people, and their culture.

GEOGRAPHY

VIETNAM HAS BEEN KNOWN by as many as 11 different names. The first name, recorded about 4,000 years ago, was Van Lang. During the Trieu dynasty (207–111 B.C.) the country was known as Nam Viet. _Nam_ means south and _viet_ means beyond or far. The Viet ethnic group is believed to be the ancestors of the Vietnamese. The name Vietnam was adopted in 1802 and used for three decades. It reappeared only as recently as 1945.

Vietnam is a long, narrow country shaped like an elongated "S" that resembles a set of scales balancing two baskets of rice. At its narrowest point, the distance between its border with Laos in the west and the South China Sea in the east is only 31 miles (50 km).

With a total area of 127,212 square miles (329,566 square km), Vietnam spans the length of the Indochinese peninsula, stretching nearly 1,000 miles (1,609 km) from north to south. It takes two days by train to travel from Hanoi in the north to Ho Chi Minh City in the south.

Vietnam's indented eastern coastline extends from the Gulf of Tonkin to the South China Sea, past the Mekong delta, and reaches the Gulf of Thailand. Forests cover 38 percent of Vietnam. There are two main areas for cultivation—the Red River delta and the Mekong delta. These two delta regions and the narrow coastal plains cover about 35 percent of the country, while the rest of the land is hilly or mountainous.

Opposite: **A boat draws near a limestone cave at Ha Long Bay.**

Below: **Dense vegetation crowds close to a house on the bank of the Mekong River. Residents depend on river and rain water for their daily needs.**

THREE GEOGRAPHIC REGIONS

Vietnam has three distinct geographic regions: Trung Bo, the middle region, consists of the Truong Son Mountains, the central highlands, and the coastal plains; Bac Bo, the north, is characterized by the Hoang Lien Mountains and the Red River delta; and Nam Bo, the south, covers the great expanse of the Mekong delta.

TRUNG BO Rising 6,500 feet (1,980 m) above sea level, the Truong Son Mountains, also known as the Annamese Cordillera, stretch 700 miles (1,100 km) from north to south, effectively separating the middle region of Vietnam from Laos and Cambodia.

The central highlands lie south of the Truong Son Mountains. Many of Vietnam's hill people, including the Ra De and Jarai, live there. They are still referred to in English as Montagnards or Highlanders, a name given to them by the French colonists.

The hill people practice slash-and-burn agriculture, cultivating dry rice (a variety that does not require immersion in water for growth), corn, black beans, and sweet potatoes. They now also grow cash crops such as coffee, tea, and medicinal plants in an effort to reduce the spread of slash-and-burn agriculture. To ease population pressure in the overcrowded urban areas, the government set up new economic zones in the central highlands. However, the scale of the resulting migration to the highlands

The Central Highlands, with a cool climate, lakes, and waterfalls, are a favorite vacation spot.

8

Deck chairs line Nha
Trang Beach.

sparked anger among the region's indigenous hill tribes that triggered a wave of violent protests. An army crackdown and an exodus of refugees to Cambodia followed.

Between the Truong Son Mountains and the South China Sea is a narrow strip of land known as the coastal plains. With the exception of Da Lat, the cities of the central region hug the coast: Hue, the imperial city during the Nguyen dynasty; Da Nang, Vietnam's fourth largest city and a seaport for neighboring Laos; and Nha Trang, a fishing port for trawlers bringing in lobster, mackerel, tuna, cuttlefish, and abalone.

The island of Hon Tre near Nha Trang is famous for its swifts' nests, which are collected and processed into a culinary delicacy. South of Nha Trang is Cam Ranh Bay, the site of a deep-water port, a shipyard, and an airbase built by the United States.

BAC BO Bac Bo is the birthplace of Vietnamese civilization. The province of Ha Son Binh, 38 miles (61 km) southwest of Hanoi, is the site of the Bronze Age settlement of Hoa Binh. Farther south, in the province of Thanh Hoa, are several sites of the Dong Son culture.

In the northwest is the Hoang Lien mountain range, where Vietnam's highest mountain, Fan Si Pan (10,312 feet/3,142 m), stands. The town of Lang Son in the northeast is the last railway stop before the Chinese border.

The northern landscape is dominated by rugged mountains and the rice fields of the Red River delta, which is one of the most densely settled rural areas in the world. Rice cultivation is the principal activity in this area.

The Red River spans 750 miles (1,200 km), starting in the Yunnan plateau in China and flowing through a narrow gorge before emerging in Lao Cai province in Vietnam. From this point, it makes a 250 mile (400 km)

journey past Hanoi before draining into the Gulf of Tonkin. The delta region measures 150 miles (241 km) at its widest and runs 75 miles (121 km) along the Gulf of Tonkin.

The region is crisscrossed by a network of earthen dikes. Flooding is a problem in the Red River delta. Silt deposited on the riverbeds for centuries has raised the water level above the surrounding plains, and dikes have been built to prevent floods. The first dikes were built over 2,000 years ago. Subsequent dynasties repaired and added more canals to the existing network, eventually creating the present system of irrigation and flood control. The worst flooding occurs between June and October. During this period, water levels may rise 33 feet (10 m) in a day.

HANOI

Greater Hanoi is one of Vietnam's three municipalities. A municipality is an administrative unit that is governed much like a province. It usually includes an inner city and an outlying district. The other two municipalities are Greater Ho Chi Minh City in the south, and Greater Haiphong, the third largest city in Vietnam, and the industrial center of the north.

Three-quarters of Hanoi's population were evacuated by the authorities during the U.S. bombardments of North Vietnam from March 1965 to October 1968. Soon after that the city grew rapidly. Today the population of greater Hanoi, which covers 826 square miles (2,139 square km), is more than 3 million, but less than a third of that number live in the city itself.

The city was named Hanoi, meaning city in the bend of the river, in 1831, but its site has been used as the capital of Vietnam since 1010. From the time of the later Ly dynasty (1009–1225), the city was called Thang Long or city of the soaring dragon. When the French took over Hanoi in 1883, they destroyed much of the ancient city to make way for new buildings. This accounts for the look of Hanoi today—an odd but charming blend of French neoclassical buildings and broad tree-lined boulevards alongside Vietnamese pagodas and cramped markets.

The number of cars has increased rapidly in the past decade, leading to traffic jams and a competition for right-of-way among cars, motor scooters, and the dwindling ranks of bicycles. The Long Bien, Chuong Duong, and Thang Long bridges take pedestrians and city traffic across the Red River. The Long Bien Bridge is the oldest of the three and was built in 1902. It was bombed repeatedly during the Vietnam War but has been repaired and continues to serve Hanoi's residents.

HA LONG BAY

Ha Long Bay is remarkable for the 3,000-odd islets that rise steeply from the sea. Most of the islets are uninhabited outcrops of dolomite or limestone and have little or no vegetation. These outcrops are actually the peaks of an ancient seabed that have risen above sea level, just as the Swiss Alps were once part of the ocean floor. Terrain of a similar form is found in the Guilin region of China.

The Vietnamese name for the bay is Vinh Ha Long, the Descending Dragon. According to legend, this area was once dry land. Then a dragon, whose footsteps were unusually heavy, descended to earth. Wherever it stepped deep valleys formed, and when it plunged into the ocean, the seawater splashed so high that it spilled into the valleys, creating Ha Long Bay.

The water of the bay is very deep and calm, allowing large ships to sail through. Numerous islands provide shelter for the small fishing boats going to and from the South China Sea.

HO CHI MINH CITY

Although Vietnam's seat of government is in Hanoi, the largest city is Ho Chi Minh City in the south. Before 1976, Ho Chi Minh City was known as Saigon, and many people still refer to the city by its former name.

The city sits on the western bank of the Saigon River and is one of the most densely populated areas in the world, with about 6,290 people per square mile (2,387 per square km), or a total population of 5 million people over an area of 794 square miles (2,056 square km).

Ho Chi Minh City is the center of commerce in Vietnam. In Dong Khoi Street and Le Loi Boulevard, the city's prime business district, foreign companies vie for office space. The streets are lined with hotels, souvenir shops, and restaurants serving international cuisine to cater to the influx of foreigners from Europe, Taiwan, Japan, and Southeast Asian countries.

About 3 miles (5 km) west of Ho Chi Minh City is the Cholon district, where many ethnic Chinese traders have settled in the last 200 years. Here, two large markets that stay open until the evening sell fresh vegetables, live fish, fresh fruit, electrical appliances, clothing, and even gold.

NAM BO The extremely fertile southern region lies in the huge 23,175 square mile (60,023 square km) Mekong delta. Unlike the Red River delta, the Mekong delta is filled with numerous minor tributaries and inlets that branch from the Mekong's nine great tributaries.

At 2,700 miles (4,535 km), the Mekong is the longest river in Southeast Asia. It flows through China and Tibet, then along Laos' border with Myanmar and Thailand and into Cambodia's Tonle Sap lake. The river then crosses into Vietnam, where it spreads out into nine main tributaries. The Mekong delta is also known as Cuu Long, or Nine Dragons, in reference to the major tributaries of the river.

During the monsoon season an unusual phenomenon occurs. The sheer volume of water in the Mekong River causes a backflow into the Tonle Sap Lake, so flooding in the south is not as serious as it is in the north.

The lower part of the Mekong delta is marshy and unsuitable for rice cultivation. Mangrove trees, often half-submerged, line the banks of the Mekong near its estuary in the southernmost part of Vietnam. These trees are home to a variety of wildlife.

"There is no comparison anywhere in the United States to that of 'early morning rush hour' in Ho Chi Minh City. … It is a rush hour of motorcycles, bicycles, and carts. There are no road regulations to obey, no sense of conformity. It is a street filled with two-wheeled bikes of all kinds going in all directions."

—from *The Vietnam Experience* (Mitchell Hammer, ed.)

13

ISLANDS

Numerous islands are situated in Ha Long Bay in the north, near the mouth of the Mekong River, and farther out, in the South China Sea. Cat Ba is the largest of the islands in Ha Long Bay. It is 83 miles (133 km) east of Hanoi and 19 miles (30 km) from Haiphong. The island is a designated national park where wildlife and coral reefs are protected.

Some islands off Vietnam's shores are the subjects of regional disputes. The Spratly Islands, which spread over untapped oil reserves, have been claimed by the Philippines, Malaysia, China, Taiwan, and Vietnam. In November 2002, during the Eighth Association of Southeast Asian Nations (ASEAN) Summit in Cambodia, all the claimants signed the Declaration on the Conduct of Parties in the South China Sea. This document is a first step designed to make it easier to find a solution to the disputes.

Vietnam's rights to Phu Quoc, Tho Chu, and the Paracel Islands have also been contested by neighboring countries eager for fishing grounds and oil and mineral deposits.

FAUNA

Wild cattle, bears, deer, tigers, and mongooses inhabit the forests of Vietnam. There are 275 species of mammals, 828 species of birds, 258 species of reptiles, 5,155 species of insects, and 82 species of amphibians.

There are a number of endangered animals, including the Javan rhinoceros, the Indian elephant, the douc langur, white-winged duck, collared laughing thrush, and the buff-cheeked gibbon.

FLORA

There are about 12,000 species of plants in Vietnam, 7,000 of which have already been identified. About 40 percent of the plants are native to the country. Teak, ebony, and palm trees as well as rattan and other vines can be found in the southern and central regions.

In the rural areas of the south, wild banana and coconut trees are common, while bamboo thickets mark off villages in the north.

Mangrove trees, which can survive submerged in seawater, grow in the marshes and coastal areas, and casuarina trees and coconut palms line many of the country's beaches.

CLIMATE

The three geographic regions of Vietnam experience very different weather conditions. In the south it is warm throughout the year with only two seasons: dry and wet. The temperature generally ranges from 70°F (21°C) to 88°F (31°C), except in the hottest months, from March to May, when the temperature can reach 95°F (35°C). In rural areas, people wear loose-fitting clothing in order to be comfortable in the heat.

It is cooler in the northern part of the country, with temperatures ranging from 58°F (14°C) to 90°F (32°C). The winter months, from November to April, are cool and dry, but the summer months, from July to November, tend to be hot and humid.

Between July and November, those living in the central coastal plains face violent typhoons. Sweeping in from the South China Sea, the storms hit the coast, causing severe damage and taking lives. The central highlands, the wettest region, receive an average of 130 inches (330 cm) of rainfall a year, compared to averages of 72 inches (183 cm) in the north and 81 inches (206 cm) in the south.

A douc langur clutches its baby. In Vietnam douc langurs live in the central highlands.

HISTORY

THE EARLIEST KNOWN civilization in Vietnam dates back to the Paleolithic age. About 300,000 years ago, migrants from southern China and eastern Indochina settled in the Black River Valley at Dong Son, southwest of present-day Hanoi. By 3,000 B.C. the Lac Viet, or People of the Valley, had developed sophisticated skills in bronze casting. The community expanded, and gradually the people moved south and settled in the Red River delta and other parts of Vietnam.

At various times, the Vietnamese waged battles against invaders from China and the ancient kingdoms of Champa and Khmer. In turn, Vietnam invaded its neighbors, gaining tribute from Laos and sovereignty over parts of Cambodia.

In 1858 Vietnam was invaded by the French, who colonized the country for nearly a century. This was followed by a long struggle for independence that culminated in the First Indochina War (1946–54). The Vietnam War (1955–75) was a struggle between North and South Vietnam.

THE KINGDOM OF VAN LANG

Ancient Vietnamese texts tell of an extraordinary man who used magical powers to unite the People of the Valley. It is believed that he established the kingdom of Van Lang in present-day Vietnam and taught the people to till the soil. Until recently, it was assumed that his successors, the Hung kings, were a mythical dynasty. However, archeological records show that a king named Lac Long did in fact live in a region in northern Vietnam known as Van Lang.

Opposite: **One of the nine dynastic urns, seen from inside the temple at Hue.**

Below: **Vietnamese in combat. Throughout history, the most characteristic feature of the Vietnamese has been a determination to preserve their independence.**

The people of Van Lang, like today's coastal Vietnamese, relied heavily on fish to supplement their diet, which consisted mainly of rice.

THE INHABITANTS The people of Van Lang were rice farmers and skilled bronze workers. They were also engaged in fishing and cattle-raising and practiced crafts such as weaving and pottery-making.

In the third century B.C., Van Lang was defeated by the neighboring state of Thuc. The restless climate among the warring states caused the king of Thuc to build a great citadel known as Co Loa, meaning Shell City, because of its shell-shaped ramparts. Despite these defensive measures, Co Loa was subject to frequent attacks in the following centuries, resulting in the eventual takeover of northern Vietnam by China in 111 B.C.

THE LEGEND OF 100 SONS

Four thousand years ago, according to Vietnamese legend, Lac Long Quan, the Dragon Lord of the Lac people, married the fairy Au Co, a descendant of the Immortals of the High Mountains. Their 100 sons hatched from 100 eggs. The 100 sons are believed to represent the 100 Viet tribes that lived long ago in southern China and northern Vietnam.

As differences in their origins gave rise to insurmountable problems, Lac Long and Au Co decided to part. They agreed that 50 sons would follow Lac Long back to the Water Palace in the South Sea, while the other 50 would go with Au Co to the mountains in Phong Chau. At Phong Chau, the eldest son, Hung Vuong, became the first king of the Hung dynasty, ruling over the kingdom of Van Lang.

CHINESE DOMINATION

The Chinese administration soon became unpopular. Forced labor, tyrannical Chinese governors, and constant demands for tribute contributed to ill feelings toward the Chinese.

Several attempts were made to overthrow the invaders. The most famous attempt was the Hai Ba Trung rebellion (A.D. 40–43), led by two sisters, Trung Trac and Trung Nhi.

After defeating the Chinese forces, the sisters ruled the country for three years until the Chinese returned to reclaim the land. The sisters decided to throw themselves in the Hat Giang River rather than surrender.

Early Vietnamese architecture, such as the imperial city in Hue, exhibits Chinese influence, the result of many centuries of Chinese domination.

The Po Klang Garai structure in Phan Rang is a remnant of the time when the Champa kingdom existed in Vietnam.

REVOLTS The majority of subsequent revolts were crushed until finally, in 939, Vietnamese forces led by Ngo Quyen defeated the Chinese in the Battle of Bach Dang River, freeing Vietnam from foreign power. After Ngo Quyen died in 944, civil war plagued the country until in 968, when Dinh Bo Linh managed to pacify the people and became king. Soon Dinh's diplomatic ties with China resulted in Vietnam becoming a Chinese vassal state. Chinese troops and administrators withdrew in exchange for Vietnam's agreement to adopt China's legal system, foreign policy, and lunar calendar. A tribute was sent every three years on condition China recognize Vietnamese independence. Through these negotiations, Dinh Bo Linh ensured Vietnamese sovereignty until the arrival of the French in the 17th century.

The long period of Chinese domination influenced Vietnamese culture. The Vietnamese adopted Chinese techniques of dike construction, rice cultivation, and animal husbandry. Knowledge of Chinese language led to Chinese influence on Vietnamese ideas about science, medicine, education, and Confucianism. An observer once suggested that Vietnam has adopted Confucianism with even greater earnestness than China. Interestingly, despite extended Chinese domination, a uniquely Vietnamese identity is still in evidence today.

VIETNAM'S GOLDEN AGE

Eleven dynasties ruled Vietnam between the 10th and mid-20th centuries. Although Vietnam remained independent, the history of this period is marked by battles with its neighbors—the Chams, Khmers, and Chinese. In A.D. 1400, a struggle for power between a weak Vietnamese king and General Ho Quy Ly allowed Chinese forces to invade and establish a Chinese government in Hanoi. Vietnam's people and resources were once again exploited to benefit China.

THE LATER LE DYNASTY Le Loi, a wealthy man from the landowning class in Thanh Hoa, organized a resistance movement against the Chinese. When the Ming government heard of the movement, it dispersed the rebels. Le Loi fled to the mountains where he and his troops had time to rest and regroup. This strengthened the movement, and in 1426 the rebel forces scored a major victory at Sontay. In 1427 they were again victorious at Lam Son, defeating China and allowing Vietnam to reclaim its independence.

Le became Emperor Le Thai To, the founder of the Later Le dynasty (1428–1527), regarded as the golden age of Vietnam. The dynasty is named Later Le in order to distinguish it from the earlier Le dynasty (980–1009).

During the Later Le, a universal system of education was established. Previously education had been limited to the sons of civil officers. The penal code was rewritten, providing greater equality, and the country was organized into systematic administrative units.

Names of successful candidates in the imperial examination are engraved on stone tablets preserved in Van Mieu, the Temple of Literature. The honor roll goes as far back as the 11th century.

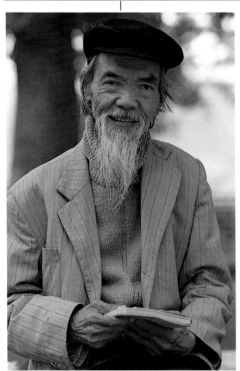

Many older, educated Vietnamese speak fluent French in addition to their native language.

THE FRENCH IN VIETNAM

French colonization of Vietnam occurred in two phases. Between 1859 and 1862, the French occupied Saigon and the surrounding area in the Mekong delta. In 1883 they annexed Hanoi and the Tonkin region.

The early years of French occupation were harsh. French officials sent to the colony were ignorant of Vietnamese traditions and sought to change the country socially, politically, and economically. Vietnamese court officials (mandarins) were forced to report to the colonial masters rather than to the Vietnamese king. To pay for the high cost of colonial administration, taxes on salt, opium, alcohol, and land were collected, and a system of forced labor known as *corvée* (korh-VAY) was established. The peasants staged uprisings in protest. Nationalists such as De Tham organized guerrilla groups, but these were swiftly and brutally put down by the French military authorities.

Jean Marie Antoine de Lanessan, governor-general of Vietnam from 1891 to 1894, published a controversial book, *La Colonisation Française en Indo-Chine*, describing the inhumane treatment of the Vietnamese during the colonial era. Prominent opponents to these acts of cruelty forced the French government to relent and encourage a more humane administration under subsequent governor-generals: Paul Doumer, Paul Beau, and Albert Sarraut. By the early 20th century, the new education system had produced a class of French-educated Vietnamese. Many of them went to universities in Paris and returned to Vietnam disillusioned by the discrimination they faced there.

NATIONALISM AND HO CHI MINH

In the early 20th century many nationalist groups were formed in Vietnam. The first of these was Quang Phuc Hoi (Association for the Restoration of Vietnam), founded in 1913 by Phan Boi Chau. After organizing several protests, Phan and other members were imprisoned. In the 1920s, the nationalist movement made an appeal to the French to provide Vietnam with a constitution. The appeal was ignored.

Little was achieved until the time of Ho Chi Minh. Born Nguyen Sinh Cung on May 19, 1890, in the province of Vinh, he worked at various jobs until he landed a job as a cook on a ship. Working on the ship he traveled to North America, Europe, and Africa. While abroad, he organized several independence movements including the Indochinese Communist Party (ICP). The French police traced him in Hong Kong, but he escaped to southern China and set up the League for the Independence of Vietnam, whose members were known as Vietminh. He returned to Vietnam in 1941 after 30 years abroad to take part in the fight for independence.

Ho Chi Minh. His life story is the story of the Vietnamese struggle for an independent and unified country.

When the Japanese invaded during World War II, the Vietminh led resistance movements against them. In 1945, with Allied victory imminent, the Japanese declared Vietnam independent from France and handed power to Emperor Bao Dai. This decision was unpopular with the Vietminh, who promptly formed a government with Ho Chi Minh as president. The emperor abdicated and Ho Chi Minh officially proclaimed Vietnam's independence on September 2, 1945.

American soldiers in a village in Vietnam. During the Vietnam War, many rural people were resettled in strategic hamlets in an effort to control Vietcong activity.

WAR IN VIETNAM

Despite protests from Vietnamese nationalists, the French returned to a governing role after World War II. Although the French met with armed resistance from the Vietminh, they received support from the Chinese Kuomintang nationalists, who recognized French sovereignty in Vietnam.

Conflict between the Vietminh and the French grew increasingly bitter, with one act of violence following another. After the shelling of Haiphong, which killed 6,000 Vietnamese in November 1946, peaceful negotiations ended. Vietnamese responded to Ho Chi Minh's call: "Let him who has a rifle use his rifle, let him who has a sword use his sword. And let those who have no sword take up pickaxes and sticks."

In 1954 Ho's brilliant strategist, Vo Nguyen Giap, led the Vietminh to victory in the decisive Battle of Dien Bien Phu. It was decided at the subsequent Geneva Conference to temporarily divide Vietnam into two states at latitude 17°N. The north was controlled by President Ho Chi Minh, while the south was controlled by President Ngo Dinh Diem. An election was to be held at the first opportunity to unite the two states, but this never occurred. Historians note that support for Ho Chi Minh was so strong at the time that he would probably have won the election.

President Diem's continual delay of the elections and the people's anger at his failure to implement necessary land and social reforms led to the Vietnam War. He was assassinated in 1963.

For two decades, Vietnam was embroiled in a civil war that devastated both north and south. U.S. involvement in Vietnam began in the 1950s, at a time when many Asian countries were trying to gain independence from their colonial rulers. The communists had just defeated the Kuomintang in China, and the Vietminh had sought assistance from Communist China. Non-communist countries were alarmed by the possibility that nationalists in other countries might be supported either by communist China or the Soviet Union.

THE DOMINO THEORY AND U.S. INVOLVEMENT

In 1954 U.S. President Dwight D. Eisenhower compared the spread of communism in Southeast Asia to a row of dominoes: "You knock over the first one, and what will happen to the last one is the certainty that it will go over very quickly."

Until 1949 the United States was reluctant to respond to French requests for intervention in Indochina. However, the ousting of the Kuomintang in China by Mao Zedong triggered fears that communism would spread. It was widely believed that if South Vietnam fell, Thailand, Laos, Burma, Cambodia, and even India and Japan would also fall to communism.

The Vietnam War became a losing battle for the United States because President Diem and his successor President Nguyen Van Thieu had little support from the South Vietnamese people. Both were dictators who reneged on promises of land redistribution and economic development.

In addition, U.S. forces were not able to differentiate between the civilian population and the Vietcong (members of the National Liberation Front of the South, allied to Ho Chi Minh's government). The destruction continued for several years and during that time more and more southerners shifted their support to the Vietcong forces.

The success of the North Vietnamese Tet offensive of 1968, the strengthening of guerrilla bases in the south, and the growing unpopularity of the war in the United States finally led to the U.S. decision to withdraw from Vietnam.

Saigon did not fall, however, until 1975. In July 1976, North and South Vietnam were reunified, and the country was renamed the Socialist Republic of Vietnam. Saigon became Ho Chi Minh City.

Refugees crossing the Perfume River in Hue, which is located near the coast in central Vietnam. Many fled Vietnam after the war. Some feared political persecution, while others left out of desperation in the face of famine and poverty.

THE BOAT PEOPLE

The Vietnam War came to an abrupt end in 1975, but many Americans had begun questioning the purpose of the war long before then. North and South Vietnamese alike were traumatized by a war that had crippled the economy and devastated the country. People looked forward to the day when they could be safely reunited with surviving family members. The long years of waking up to bomb explosions and the cries of injured children had taken its toll. When the National Liberation Force (Vietcong) took Saigon in April 1975, there was little resistance from the Army of the Republic of Vietnam.

Following reunification, several religious leaders, politicians, intellectuals, and union leaders were imprisoned and reeducated (taught to abide by the views of the new Vietnamese regime). Many who had served or supported the Saigon government escaped and took refuge in other countries. This was the beginning of the first wave of refugees known as the boat people.

The long war had severely disrupted the economy. Essential goods such as rice had to be imported. Intensive bombing and the use of defoliants, such as Agent Orange, had turned much of the country into a wasteland, and land had to be recultivated. Inflation and unemployment soared, and health care was inadequate. Faced with such conditions, thousands of economic refugees set sail from the inlets of the Mekong delta in search of better conditions.

WAR IN CAMBODIA

To add to the country's woes, the Chinese-backed Khmer Rouge of Cambodia invaded Vietnam in 1977. In retaliation, Vietnam, with Soviet backing, entered Cambodia in 1978 and set up a Vietnamese-supported government under Heng Samrin. Although the invasion was widely condemned, the Heng Samrin regime put a stop to Pol Pot's genocidal rampage. The Vietnamese invasion alienated the West even further and led to an international boycott of Vietnamese goods.

It is only since 1990, when the last of the Vietnamese troops were withdrawn from Cambodia, that Vietnam reestablished trade and diplomatic ties with its Asian neighbors.

The United States' trade embargo on Vietnam that began in 1975 was finally repealed in 1994 during President Bill Clinton's term, despite protests from U.S. Vietnam War veterans. Both countries are currently attempting to normalize relations.

A satellite dish in Ho Chi Minh City. After half a century of struggle, Vietnamese look forward to peace and development.

GOVERNMENT

THE SOCIALIST REPUBLIC OF VIETNAM is a Communist state with exclusive power held by the Communist Party of Vietnam (CPV). Vietnam's constitution was first written in 1980 and revised in 1992. The later version reduced the role of the Communist Party and made the president head of state. There are three branches of government: the legislative, represented by the National Assembly; the executive, made up of the president and a cabinet of ministers; and the judiciary, represented by the Supreme People's Court. The president is elected to a five-year term by the National Assembly.

THE NATIONAL ASSEMBLY

The Vietnamese legislature, the "highest organ of State power," is responsible for drafting the consitution, proposing and enacting laws, and approving the annual budget and the five-year socioeconomic plans. Regional and provincial issues are the responsibility of the designated ministries, state committees, and special government bodies.

Apart from managing internal affairs, the National Assembly has also been developing Vietnam's international relationships by participating in foreign and international bodies, such as the Asia-Pacific Parliamentary Forum (APPF) and International Parliamentary Union (IPU).

The National Assembly consists of 498 members who are elected to five-year terms by all citizens over 18 years of age. The Assembly was formed on January 6, 1946 after the first general election in the country, and it approved Vietnam's first constitution on November 9 that same year.

Opposite: **A statue of Ho Chi Minh is located outside the City Hall in Ho Chi Minh City, Vietnam.**

Below: **A statue of Lenin in Hanoi. The philosophies of Karl Marx and Vladimir Ilich Lenin have shaped Vietnam's ideology.**

Vietnamese policemen play an important role in maintaining law and order in the country.

THE CABINET

The cabinet, headed by the prime minister, is responsible for the functions of the ministries, government departments, state committees in the cities, and people's committees in the provinces. A province is divided into districts, each with its own people's council. District elections are held once every two years to vote in a new council.

With the National Assembly's backing, the prime minister may select and reject members of the cabinet. The prime minister may also annul or suspend decisions or directives issued by the ministries.

THE JUDICIAL SYSTEM

Vietnam's legal system is based on French laws but has been modified to fit communist legal theory. The president of the Supreme People's Court, which presides over the Court of Appeal and the people's and military courts at the provincial level, answers to the National Assembly.

A new penal code enacted in 1989 provides for some legal reforms but retains the death penalty. Further amendments to the penal code passed by the National Assembly in 1992 have increased the penalties for economic crimes. Serious cases of bribe-taking, counterfeiting, fraud, theft of state property, as well as treason and espionage, are now considered capital offences punishable by death. As economic development has accelerated in Vietnam, so has the growth of corruption.

THE CONSTITUTION

All government and legislative authority in Vietnam is derived from the constitution. The Democratic Republic and, later, Socialist Republic have had four constitutions, the latest drafted in 1992.

FIRST CONSTITUTION The first constitution was drafted in 1946, one year after independence was declared in North Vietnam. Inspired by the constitutions of France and the United States, the 1946 constitution reflects the ideals of the newly independent state, such as individual rights, equality, freedom, and independence.

The Child Care, Protection, and Education Law (1991) lays down a number of basic rights for all Vietnamese, including the right to own and inherit property.

SECOND CONSTITUTION The second constitution was drafted in 1959, after it became apparent that elections would not be held throughout Vietnam as planned, and that North and South Vietnams would remain divided for the immediate future. The second constitution declared the goals of the Democratic Republic of Vietnam in creating a communist society characterized by central planning and collective property ownership.

31

THIRD CONSTITUTION After reunification in 1976, it was necessary to draft a new constitution. The 1980 constitution called for the rapid collectivization of property and emphasized the dominant role of the Communist Party, declaring it to be the main factor in determining the success of the Vietnamese revolution.

FOURTH CONSTITUTION Between 1986 and 1989, the government introduced a series of economic reforms. The constitution drafted in 1992 defines Vietnam as a multisector market economy, meaning that state, collective, and private enterprise are recognized as different but essential parts of the economy. Although the newly introduced reforms have produced favorable results for the economy, Vietnam's leaders are still divided over how to maintain a balance between a market-based economy and a socialist state.

Do Muoi, who served as the CPV secretary-general until 1997, is a veteran of the struggle for independence.

COMMUNIST PARTY OF VIETNAM

The political system is dominated by the Communist Party of Vietnam (CPV), or Dang Cong San Viet Nam. Founded in 1930 by Ho Chi Minh, the party has a collective leadership, and the governing body of about 150 members is known as the Central Committee. The CPV has more than two million members and continues to recruit more.

The Politburo is the power center of the Communist Party. The 13-member bureau formulates the country's social and economic goals as well as the party's political direction.

VIETNAM'S LEADERS

President Tran Duc Luong joined the CPV in 1959 and rose through the political ranks to be elected the president of Vietnam in 1997. He was reelected president in August 2002. Phan Van Khai was also reelected prime minister for another five years in the same elections.

Tran's predecessors were Ho Chi Minh, Vo Chi Cong, and General Le Duc Anh. Along with Prime Minister Phan Van Khai and other members of the Politburo, Tran has put measures in place to help Vietnam grow to be fully industrialized by 2020.

Earlier leaders set the groundwork for Tran's success. Prime Minister Phan Van Khai, who was then only a member of the Politburo, joined forces with other members in the 1980s and 1990s, such as Do Muoi, Le Phuoc Tho, Bui Thien Ngo, and Vo Tran Chi, to accelerate economic growth and develop the country's infrastructure, especially in the areas of telecommunications and water and power supply. They were also instrumental in transforming Vietnam from a country on the point of starvation in the 1980s to one that has become the world's second largest exporter of rice and that achieved a growth rate of 7 percent in 2003.

Vietnam's prime minister, Phan Van Khai.

With this as a foundation, the current leaders of Vietnam have made significant progress in bringing the country into the 21st century. In recent years, there has been a move away from the planned economic model and toward a more effective market-based economic system, resulting in increased international trade relations.

ECONOMY

VIETNAM'S ECONOMY is predominantly agricultural. Vietnamese authorities have introduced measures to modernize the economy and encourage export-driven industries. As a result, agriculture accounted for only 24 percent of the gross domestic product (GDP) in 2003 as compared to 30 percent in 1993. The labor force involved in agriculture also declined from 70 percent in 1993 to 63 percent in 2003, although the proportion is still rather large compared to other areas of the economy.

The fertile Red River and Mekong deltas supply the country with rice, the staple food. Fishing and forestry, although relatively small industries, provide fresh fish and lumber.

THE POST-WAR ECONOMY

Colonialism and two very long wars left Vietnam severely impoverished. During the Vietnam War, agricultural activity throughout the country was disrupted, and South Vietnam relied heavily on U.S. subsidies and imported goods. Collective farming after the war initially produced poor results, and even though production gradually improved, the lack of infrastructure and foreign aid, a low level of exports, runaway inflation, and unemployment led to a near-famine situation in 1980. In 1979 Vietnam's invasion of Cambodia led to an embargo on foreign aid and trade from the United States and its allies. Many other countries joined the embargo, and Vietnam had to rely on subsidies from the Soviet bloc to fund state enterprises. Vietnam's imports far exceeded exports.

Opposite: **A man works in a rice field. Rice is planted on 75 percent of cultivated land in Vietnam.**

Below: **A Vietnamese boat family whose main occupation is fishing.**

A MARKET ECONOMY

By 1985, despite its vast natural resources, Vietnam was one of the poorest countries in the world. Among the problems it faced were inflation, foreign debt, a shortage of raw materials for industry, a limited supply of consumer goods, and unemployment. In 1986 the Soviet Union announced that it could no longer provide economic assistance to Vietnam. Vietnamese leaders introduced a radical economic reform program known as *doi moi* (doy moy), or renovation. The policy encourages production in the private sector, agriculture, and light industries.

ECONOMIC REFORMS

Beginning in 1986, state subsidies to factories were cut, incentives for individual productivity increased, and state guarantees for salaries gradually removed. Collective farming was modified and private enterprise permitted. The government also made efforts to improve the country's infrastructure in order to lure foreign investment.

The complete removal of the trade embargo on Vietnam in 1995 opened the doors to more foreign investment and general interest in enterprise. In 2000 Vietnam and the United States signed a bilateral trade agreement, which greatly increased two-way trade between the two countries.

The Asian financial crisis of 1997 affected many Asian countries including Vietnam. Despite this, Vietnam managed to achieve an annual growth of 7 percent in 2002. In 2003 Vietnam hosted the South East Asian (SEA) Games for the first time. This benefited several areas of the economy, tourism and retail in particular.

Lang Son, Vietnam's gateway to China. The government's economic reforms are designed to increase foreign investment, and Vietnam is now reopening its doors to the world.

SOURCES OF REVENUE Vietnam's income comes from the export of rice, crude oil, coffee, and rubber. Tourism, mining, and forestry are being developed to contribute to foreign exchange. Imports include fertilizer, petroleum products, and machinery and equipment. Vietnam's major trade partners are the United States, Japan, Australia, China, Germany, Singapore, and the United Kingdom for exports and South Korea, China, Japan, Singapore, Taiwan, and Thailand for imports.

AGRICULTURE

Agriculture remains the basis of Vietnam's economy, accounting for 22 percent of total land area in use. Rice, the primary crop, accounts for 75 percent of all cultivated land.

Other food crops are corn, cassava, sweet potatoes, sugarcane, and potatoes. Cereals, such as millet and lentils, are also cultivated along with vegetables, including snow peas, beans, tomatoes, okra, cabbage, and carrots.

Bananas are the most commonly cultivated fruit, but the fertile land also yields mangoes, lychees, pineapples, watermelons, sapodillas, breadfruit, milk fruit, and green dragon fruit. Strawberries and citrus fruits are grown in the cooler parts of the country.

The most important cash crops are rubber, tea, coffee, tobacco, and pepper, but farmers also obtain income from growing various herbs used in traditional Vietnamese and other Asian medicines.

The Foreign Trade Bank in Hanoi. The government has drafted new banking and investment laws to cope with the new economy.

A Vietnamese working at a cotton mill. The textile industry has grown considerably since the implementation of *doi moi.*

FISHING AND FOREST PRODUCE

Vietnam's long coastline and numerous small lakes and rivers make seafood one of the country's major exports. Shrimp, lobster, abalone, crab, shellfish, tuna, mackerel, and snapper are among the many kinds of fish that can be found in Vietnamese waters.

The forests provide bamboo, cinnamon, lacquer (from the son tree), resin, and quinine (from the cinchona tree). Vietnam's rainforests form a natural barrier that protects the agricultural lowlands from flooding during the rainy season, and efforts are ongoing to replace forests lost to war and overlogging.

MINING AND MANUFACTURING

Vietnam has substantial deposits of oil, coal, bauxite, phosphates, iron, lead, zinc, tin, and wolfram. It also has smaller deposits of manganese, graphite, titanium, gold, rare earth, and precious and semiprecious stones. Other than gold, oil, and coal, these minerals have only been extracted in small quantities. In 1998 the government entered joint ventures with foreign companies to exploit its mineral resources. Oilfields in the South China Sea now produce over 80,000 barrels of oil a day.

Manufacturing represented 37 percent of Vietnam's GDP in 2003. Most of the country's heavy industries were developed in the 1950s. They include steel, cement, food processing, textile manufacturing, and cotton mills. Light industries produce daily necessities such as bicycles, farm tools, and domestic utensils.

Bicycles, three-wheeled taxis, and other smaller vehicles crowd each other in the early morning rush hour in the city.

INFRASTRUCTURE

The government has established special export processing zones (EPZs) in Hanoi, Ho Chi Minh City, Da Nang, and Can Tho, all locations of joint ventures between Vietnamese and foreign companies. The EPZs service labor-intensive, export-oriented light industries, such as electronics, plastics, and seafood processing.

POWER Vietnam is dependent on hydroelectric power for at least 56 percent of its electricity and is subject to regular power cuts during the dry season, with officials routinely encouraging urban centers such as Ho Chi Minh City and Hanoi to cut private consumption. There are nine hydropower plants of various sizes. Construction of more dams has become a point of debate as many people have to be resettled.

TRANSPORTATION Vietnam's international airports are Noi Ba in Hanoi and Tan Son Nhat in Ho Chi Minh City. Railroad tracks, which total 1,953 miles (3,142 km), connect major cities and coastal towns. Vietnam's largest seaport is Haiphong. Other major port cities include Da Nang, Quy Nhon, and Ho Chi Minh City.

Dried rice noodles being taken to market. Small business enterprise such as the manufacture and trade of traditional goods is increasing.

VIETNAM'S WORKFORCE

Vietnam has a workforce of about 39 million. Each city and provincial area has a different per capita income. The proportion of people with per capita income below the poverty line has dropped dramatically, from 58 percent in 1993 to 37 percent in 1998. Of these, 15 percent live below the food poverty line. Vietnam faces a problem with unemployment, with 25 percent of its population jobless.

Vietnamese are hardworking and earnest, highly literate, and eager to be trained and to further their education.

In the old collective system, agricultural workers were paid partly in cash and partly in coupons, which could be exchanged for rice and other basic items. Payment was based on the amount of work a person did as well as his or her service to the party. Factory workers, teachers, doctors, and military officers received very much the same pay. Today, income varies according to whether one works in a foreign company or a state-owned enterprise. *Doi moi* has also produced some wealthy private entrepreneurs. Growing economic inequality is a topic of much concern in both public and private discussions.

ENTREPRENEURSHIP

Before 1986 small family-owned businesses were not permitted by the government. Between 1989 and 1995 almost half of Vietnam's state-owned enterprises were either closed down or privatized, that is, leased to an investor.

Other state enterprises have given employees and the public the opportunity to purchase shares.

Electronics and other industries are concentrated in EPZs in Vietnam.

TOURISM

In the early 1990s the number of tourists and business visitors surged after Vietnam opened its doors, and more hotels were built to accommodate these visitors. In 2003, the year that the Severe Acute Respiratory Syndrome (SARS) broke out, foreign visitor arrivals in Vietnam dropped by 15 percent compared to the previous year. The decrease could have been worse, but luckily for Vietnam it was credited as the first country in the world to successfully contain SARS. The decrease was also offset by arrivals during the 22nd SEA Games, held in Hanoi in December 2003.

ENVIRONMENT

VIETNAM HAS EXPERIENCED a lot of change since it began to industrialize and modernize its economy. Accelerated economic development has brought the Vietnamese a higher standard of living but has also threatened the country's resources and environment. Vietnam periodically suffers from serious flooding, and is facing a population boom and many of the problems associated with industrialization. In addition, studies show that Agent Orange still contaminates Vietnam.

AGENT ORANGE

Agent Orange is a herbicide used by the U.S. military during the Vietnam War to destroy foliage that the enemy could hide in. Agent Orange (a code name derived from the orange band marked around the drums storing the chemical) is a combination of two chemicals and was used as a weed killer in the 1940s. The U.S. military sprayed 20 million gallons (76 million liters) of herbicides over Vietnam from 1961 to 1971.

Early health studies showed that Agent Orange contained dioxin, which caused many diseases in animals, mostly fatal. It was later found that Agent Orange was harmful to humans as well.

A study in 2001 showed that blood and water samples, sediment, and soil collected in southern Vietnam contained high levels of dioxin. This meant that Agent Orange was still present in Vietnam in a limited number of areas that were heavily and repeatedly sprayed, such as the perimeters of former military bases. People living in those areas continue to be at risk of dioxin contamination.

Even though the spraying stopped decades ago, Agent Orange is in the food chain because it has settled into the soil and water. It contaminates ducks, fish, and plants, which are consumed by people.

Agent Orange can cause prostate, respiratory, and lymphatic cancers in people who are exposed to the chemical. The children of people who are exposed to Agent Orange can have birth defects such as a cleft palate, extra fingers or toes, or spina bifida, a condition in which the spinal cord is not properly protected by the vertebral column.

Opposite: **Rocky islets rise up from the water on a calm day at Ha Long Bay.**

NATURAL RESOURCES

WATER Vietnam's waters suffer from pollution and an ecological imbalance due to human activity.

Industrial activity is increasing rapidly, but the facilities to cope with industrial waste disposal have not developed at the same rate. As a result, waste containing heavy metals and acids flows into rivers and the sea. The same is true for agricultural waste. In the cities most solid waste produced by the general population is not collected but is instead dumped in or near bodies of water. Stream and river erosion due to deforestation aggravates water pollution.

Overfishing, fishing with poisons or explosives, and agricultural pesticide run-offs have upset the ecological balance in Vietnam's waters. Coral reefs are damaged by these activities as well as by coral mining to feed the souvenir trade.

In addition, Vietnam has an inadequate water supply for its people. Less than half of urban residents had access to clean water in 2000. Figures were lower for rural residents. This water shortage is mainly due to the lack of infrastructure to tap the full potential of rivers running through the country. Rainfall is also unevenly distributed throughout the year with prolonged dry spells.

AIR Industrialization and modernization have also affected air quality in Vietnam. Most urban areas are polluted by dust. Construction activities account for a large portion of this dust. Hanoi and Ho Chi Minh City in particular suffer from pollution by industrial emissions. Many residential areas are located near industrial areas and main roads, and so large numbers of people are exposed to the pollutants. This has led to health problems such as respiratory diseases. Air pollution has also decreased the yield and quality of agricultural output.

The use of leaded gasoline in vehicles adds to air pollution in Vietnam.

LAND Deforestation due to logging, forest fires, war, shifting cultivation, collection of firewood, and overgrazing has greatly reduced Vietnam's forested area and caused serious soil erosion. In 1945 forests covered 43 percent of Vietnam's total land area, but this dropped to only 27 percent in 1995.

Many individual plant and animal species are endangered as a result of overhunting, wildlife trade, war, and overutilization. Deforestation and expanding human settlements have broken up extended wildlife habitats into small pockets. These may not be big enough to sustain large or wide-ranging animals. Endangered species in Vietnam include the black-faced spoonbill, douc langurs, and golden Vietnamese cypress.

Above: Cash crops such as rubber trees were used in Vietnam's replanting programs.

Opposite: The National Strategy for Environmental Protection aims to collect 90 percent of solid garbage and dispose of more than 60 percent of dangerous rubbish and all hospital waste.

ENVIRONMENTAL IMPROVEMENTS

Vietnam recognized the importance of taking care of the environment and took conservation steps as early as 1962 when it established the Cuc Phuong National Park, its first nature reserve. Since then the country has enacted laws and launched projects that benefit the environment.

SAVING THE FORESTS To address the problem of deforestation, the Vietnamese government introduced the Regreening the Barren Hills project in 1992. The project was designed to reforest open land, barren hills, and mountains, while protecting the forests. A total of about 22.2 million acres (9 million hectares) of forest were improved and protected in this program. It was followed by the Five-Million-Hectare Reforestation Program in 1998, designed to reforest 12.4 million acres (5 million hectares) of land in Vietnam by 2010 by natural regeneration and replanting. Cash crops and fruit trees are involved in the replanting programs.

Vietnam has also developed a protected areas system, which consists of national parks, nature reserves, and protected landscapes. The country has also banned logging in most production forests, which are developed for commercial exploitation, and decreased the number of state-run forestry companies.

WILDLIFE TRADE Vietnam became party to the Convention of International Trade in Endangered Species of Wild Fauna and Flora (CITES) in 1994. People who trade, import, or export wild animals and plants are required to obtain permits and licenses from the authorities.

provides guidelines for the management of industrial areas, major livestock raising and slaughtering areas, and garbage dumping grounds. The law also bans the discharge of industrial waste into bodies of water and recognizes that the fight against water pollution and depletion is linked with the need to address deforestation.

MULTI-PRONGED APPROACH Between 2001 and 2010, Vietnam will implement the National Strategy for Environmental Protection (NSEP), a project that addresses multiple environmental problems. The program has specific targets, such as ensuring that 95 percent of urban residents and 85 percent of rural residents have access to drinking water by 2010. More areas are expected to be marked as nature reserves, while forests will be grown on at least 40 percent of the land. Canals, ponds, and rivers in the urban areas will be upgraded. A system of garbage disposal will be implemented in households and enterprises, while trash cans will be put in public places to ensure cleanliness.

INTERNAL DIASPORA

With 82 million people, Vietnam is already one of the most densely populated countries in the world, and the population looks set to exceed the 100-million mark by 2025. The coastal areas as well as the Mekong and Red River deltas are particularly crowded.

To solve the overcrowding problem the government has encouraged people living in these areas to move to the highlands, which are less crowded. This internal migration began in the early 1980s.

The government has cleared forests in the highlands to grow cash crops, such as coffee and tea. Migrants work in new economic zones that consist of state-run farms and cooperatives.

This paddy field sits amid modern housing in Ho Chi Minh City. An expanding population and a rapid rate of urbanization have resulted in overcrowding in the lowland areas.

MONTAGNARDS   The migration has caused dissension among the Montagnards, or mountain people, of the highlands.

After the war years the government forbade the Montagnards from continuing their nomadic slash-and-burn farming practice, claiming that this practice denuded forests. The hill people had to settle down and abandon their nomadic lifestyle.

Their ancestral land was taken by the government for redistribution to the original inhabitants and settlers alike. However, the land was rarely redistributed fairly because of poor administration and corruption.

The original inhabitants of the highlands were increasingly outnumbered and displaced by the settlers, and they resented being reduced to a minority in their own land.

Large-scale coffee planting in the highlands has been so successful that

plummeted. The Montagnards, who only grow coffee as a cash crop and no longer have enough land for subsistence farming, have lost their means of livelihood.

These factors, among others, have led to uprisings by ethnic minority groups against the government. In February 2001 thousands of minority group members took to the streets in two provinces in the central highlands. Another protest of a similar scale took place earlier, in 1997, in Thai Binh province against land distribution by corrupt officials. Smaller groups of protesters also set fire to plantations and fought with local police and settlers in August 2000.

A Montagnard woman carrying a stack of firewood. The indigenous peoples in the highlands have increasingly been outnumbered by settlers from the lowlands.

VIETNAMESE

MORE THAN 85 PERCENT of Vietnam's 82 million people are descendants of the original settlers in the Red River delta region. They are known as the Viet, or Kinh, ethnic group. The Chinese, who form 2 percent of the entire population and are the second largest group, are mainly descendants of traders who settled in the Mekong delta about 200 years ago. Almost 60 different ethnic groups make up the remainder of Vietnam's population.

Overcrowding has been a problem in Vietnam since the 15th century. To control population growth, the government urged people to marry at a later age and to have only two children. Although Vietnamese in general have followed this rule, this measure alone has not been adequate. At 615 persons per square mile (237 per square km), Vietnam remains among the most densely populated countries in the world.

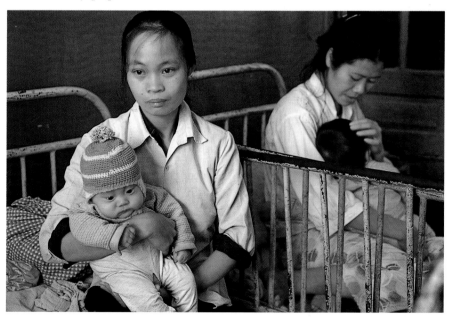

Left: **Mothers with their infants in a ward of a hospital in Hanoi. Vietnam's population is increasing at a rate of 1.29 percent every year.**

Opposite: **Young Vietnamese women in traditional dress and hat, which keeps out the sun.**

LONGER LIFE The average life expectancy has increased over the last 50 years and is now 73 years. This is mainly because the Vietnamese have improved their health services by training large numbers of doctors, nurses, midwives, and paramedics. Every district has a maternity clinic and a hospital, while each village has a health station to cope with less serious ailments. Good medical centers can be found in Hanoi and Ho Chi Minh City.

THE VIETNAMESE

In a longhouse set on stilts, an old Muong woman puffs on a bamboo pipe.

The Vietnamese are descendants of the Viet, Tai, and Chinese people who first settled in northern Vietnam over 2,000 years ago. They were dependent on rice farming and made their home in the fertile lowland and delta areas. As the population increased, the people migrated to the central coastal plains and later to the Mekong delta.

Today, the two most densely populated areas in Vietnam are still the Red River and Mekong deltas.

NORTH-SOUTH DIFFERENCES

Although the Vietnamese have thought of themselves as a single nation since Ngo Quyen drove out the Chinese rulers in A.D. 939, northerners and southerners have developed their own distinctive character. Politically, the country was divided for more than 20 years between 1954 and 1975.

A Vietnamese selling jeans and jackets in the northern city of Hanoi.

Vietnamese in the north lived under a communist government with a centrally controlled economy, while those in the south developed a capitalist economy and were exposed to a Western style of life under the influence of the U.S. bases throughout the southern half of Vietnam.

But long before the country was divided, the people of Hue and areas farther south had developed some striking regional variations. Northerners are more Confucian in their outlook on family and lifestyle. They have great regard for learning and religious rituals and a great appreciation of history and literature. Southerners tend to be more open to new ideas and more willing to take risks. Theirs is a less structured society. Their ancestors were pioneers who did not have the support of a traditional village and were not accustomed to the strict social conventions that came with Confucianism.

THE WILD SOUTH

The south in the 15th to 18th centuries was to the Vietnamese what the Wild West was to the early American settlers. The pioneers who ventured south were migrants who left home because of war or famine, or to escape victimization by unjust government officials. Some moved to avoid paying debts or taxes, while others were looking for adventure or land to homestead. When they set up their new homes in the south, they faced hostility from the Chams and raids from the highlanders. Gradually, as they settled in, the Vietnamese were influenced by the Cham culture and intermarriage occurred.

Later, French concentration on commercial activity in the south gave southerners exposure to capitalist concepts. Despite the differences between the north and south, the Vietnamese still regard themselves as a single nation.

THE CHAM

The Cham are ethnically different from the other hill peoples. They are a Malayo-Polynesian people who speak Cham, an Austronesian language. Totaling 100,000, the Cham originated in the Southeast Asian archipelago and are surviving descendants of the Champa kingdom, which lasted from the second to 17th centuries A.D.

Unlike the rest of the Vietnamese, the Cham have a culture that exhibits Indian influences. They were exposed to Buddhism and Hinduism long ago, and the influence of these religions can be seen in Cham customs, language, and script (Sanskrit). The religion commonly practiced is a modified form of Hinduism. Many of their intricate sculptural and architectural designs are manifestations of their religious beliefs. The

The port of Saigon in the south did not exist until the 14th century, when it was known as Prey Nokor. By the 18th century the Nguyen lords were governing the area under the authority of the Cambodian king.

A Tay girl. The Tay are the largest hill group in Vietnam.

Cham worship many gods, but their primary image of worship is a woman whom they regard as the mother of the country. She is believed to have given birth to the dynasties that once ruled Vietnam.

Some of the Cham are Muslims. They were introduced to Islam by Muslim traders from India, Malaysia, and Indonesia.

According to ancient scribes, the Cham were exceptionally clean and washed themselves many times a day, rubbing their bodies with a mixture of camphor and musk and anointing themselves with perfume. They are traditionally a matrilineal society.

The Cham now occupy the Phan Rang and Phan Thiet regions near the Mekong delta, and a portion of the delta along the Cambodian border.

THE HILL PEOPLES

The hills of Vietnam are populated by several groups of people, each with its own dialect, customs, dress, and way of life. Many hill peoples practice an animistic form of worship. Some have been converted by missionaries and are Protestants or Roman Catholics who speak French or English in addition to their native dialect.

MONTAGNARDS The hill peoples in central and southern Vietnam were known to the French as Montagnards (mountain people), a term still used. In the past, Montagnards were enlisted as resistance fighters by the French and Americans against the Vietminh because they were traditionally anti-Vietnamese. The Montagnards include the Mnong, Ra De, Jarai, Bahnar, and Sedang peoples who reside in the high plateaus of the west.

VARIOUS GROUPS The peoples of the northern provinces include the Tay, Nung, Tai, Muong, and Hmong. The Tay live in stilt houses and cultivate crops. Unlike other hill peoples, their beliefs are influenced by Buddhism, Taoism, and Confucianism. The Nung live in the same provinces as the Tay. They cultivate the land and raise livestock. The Tai are skillful weavers and hunters. The Hmong live in the most remote areas. They raise pigs, cows, and horses and grow vegetables and fruit trees.

Cholon, the Chinatown of southern Vietnam, bustles with commerce. The Chinese are quick to capitalize on viable trades in this busy market.

THE CHINESE

The Chinese settled in the Mekong delta about 200 years ago. Before the 1970s, there was a larger community of Chinese, but many fled the country after the Communists took over Saigon and during the 1979 border clashes with China. Most Chinese live in the urban areas, such as the Cholon district of Ho Chi Minh City, where they often run small family businesses. The Chinese speak Vietnamese as well as their own dialects—Cantonese, Fukien, and Chao Zhu. Most of the older generation read and write using Chinese characters rather than *quoc ngu* (kwok noo), the Vietnamese romanized script.

OVERSEAS VIETNAMESE

Viet Kieu is the name that has been given to overseas Vietnamese, most of whom live in the United States, Canada, Europe, and Australia. As members of the Republican government, they were marked as capitalists, and along with many Catholics, they fled in the 1970s, fearing reprisals by the new communist government. After the first helicopter evacuation in 1975, many other Vietnamese left the country in small boats, sailing out into the rough South China Sea and facing great danger, including pirate attacks. Even when they reached other countries, there was no guarantee that they would be given refugee status.

Today, Vietnamese refugee camps in neighboring countries have been emptied, although there are still a handful of the *Viet Kieu* left who have not yet found a home.

DRESS

The traditional suit for men is the *ao the* (ow-TUH), and that for women is the *ao-dai* (ow-ZAI in the north and ow-YAI in the south). The *ao-dai* is a long, fitted tunic over white or black pants. The tunic is slit up to the waist on either side to allow easy movement. It is not unusual for Vietnamese women dressed in *ao-dai* to zip through the city on a motorcycle or bicycle. Men's *ao the* are similar, but the tunic is looser.

The *ao-dai* is enjoying a revival in popularity even among modern young Vietnamese.

WORKING ATTIRE Office wear is usually a short-sleeved shirt and pants for men, and a pantsuit for women. In the north, jackets are necessary during the winter months.

Older men and women in the countryside wear *ao-dai*. When working in the fields, men wear shorts or rolled-up pants. Most Vietnamese women find shorts unsightly and prefer to wear rolled-up pants when working in the rice fields.

Traditionally, high-heeled wooden sandals called *guoc* (gwok) were worn with the *ao-dai*, but today most village people wear sandals or go barefoot. Sandals or shoes are generally worn in the city, depending on the time of year.

Non la, the conical hat, is indispensable in Vietnam's hot climate.

CASUAL CLOTHES In a country that is hot for the better part of the year, the *non la* (non-lah), or conical palm hat, provides a wide brim of cooling shade. *Non la* are worn by women in the village and in the city to protect them from the intense heat of the sun. A fair complexion is an asset, so most Vietnamese women try to avoid the sun when they can.

Young people in the city dress casually when they are not at work. Both men and women wear jeans or pants, particularly since bicycles and scooters are common forms of transportation.

It is common to see young ladies in T-shirts and jeans strolling in the city or going to the movies, although some young women prefer traditional dress.

THE SOCIAL HIERARCHY

In prewar Vietnamese society, the traditional Confucian hierarchy was the norm. Mandarins and scholars were the most highly regarded, followed by peasants, tradesmen and artisans, and finally merchants—even if wealthy—at the bottom.

When the communists came into power, land owned by mandarins and other landowners was seized and redistributed, forever altering the 2,000-year-old class structure. Factory workers and peasants enjoyed the same status as doctors and professors, and professionals earned less than workers. Nevertheless, teachers and graduates were still highly respected.

Until recently, political cadres and government workers enjoyed the most benefits. But in comparison to other communist regimes, Vietnam's political leaders do not have a luxurious lifestyle. With the country's economic liberalization, businessmen and traders have made a comeback. Many people in the city, having lived in a country that has been poor for so long, aspire to be successful in business, or at least to have a well-paying office job.

Workers crammed into a lambretta. In the past, workers brought home more pay than professionals in Vietnam.

LIFESTYLE

TYPICAL SCENES IN THE Vietnamese countryside—bamboo-hedged villages, a patchwork of rice fields, and farmers with water buffalo—depict a way of life that has remained unchanged for hundreds of years. To an extent this is true, for even now four-fifths of the population live in rural areas. Yet in the past 60 years, many old customs, such as arranged marriages, polygamy, elaborate funerals, and black lacquered teeth (once regarded as beautiful and recently determined to have protective value against decay), have been downplayed.

In addition to the traditional Confucian virtues of benevolence, respect for social order, trustworthiness, determination, and care for the less fortunate, Vietnamese children are taught the importance of nationhood. The Vietnamese have traditionally been reluctant to move from their ancestral villages, but many were given no choice during the Vietnam War.

Other factors have changed the face of Vietnamese society. Industrialization has created new types of work and a different lifestyle in a country that used to depend mainly on agriculture. Couples marry later and have smaller families (two to three children, on average) in response to the government's message to keep population growth down. In the past, the average was four or five children. Compulsory elementary and adult education have increased the literacy rate by leaps and bounds, from 14 percent in 1945 to an impressive 94 percent in 2003.

Opposite: **Workers crowd the roads as they ride home on motorcycles at the end of the day.**

Below: **A state-run orphanage equips children with work skills. The girl on the right is Amerasian.**

61

Elementary education is free and compulsory for children in Vietnam.

EDUCATION

The first university was set up in Hanoi in the 11th century. Since that time Vietnamese scholars have been highly esteemed. Nevertheless, in 1930 less than one-tenth of the population was literate. In 1945 elementary schools were set up for children, and night classes were offered for adults to equip them with basic skills in reading and writing, especially in the use of *quoc ngu*, the Vietnamese romanized script. Since then an entirely new education system has been established.

Nursery school is optional, so generally children start elementary school at the age of 6. There are three cycles of education in Vietnam. The first cycle of five years is compulsory and teaches students basic skills such as reading, writing, and mathematics.

Those who have the aptitude go on to secondary school, a four-year cycle. History, geography, literature, the sciences, and a second language are taught at the secondary level. Students can choose either Russian or English as a second language. English is by far the more popular choice.

Students who complete secondary school qualify for higher education at a college or university.

Those who do not attend secondary school may continue their education at a technical or vocational institute that prepares them for a specific profession. There are also agricultural institutes where students and farmers learn about advanced farming techniques, horticulture, and animal husbandry.

Many Vietnamese hope to go to college, not only because of the traditional esteem for learning but also because they believe that a college degree is their passport to a good job in the city.

FAMILY

Despite the rapid changes of the past decades, Vietnamese have continued to regard the family as the most important institution. If one considers the number of festivals connected with honoring the dead and the number of altars in the home dedicated to ancestors, it is clear that when Vietnamese think of family, they consider not just the living but also the dead.

To a Vietnamese, nothing offers more warmth and security than the family.

.Wherever possible, three generations of a family live together in the same house. Men and women live with their parents until they marry. When it is not possible to live together, married offspring will choose to live close to their parents' house. Even if far away, the families will visit each other frequently.

The husband is acknowledged as the head of the household, and according to Confucian tradition his wife is expected to obey, respect, serve, and be faithful to him. But as most Vietnamese will admit, the wife is really the "general of the interior."

It is common for both husband and wife to work, so young children are usually looked after by their grandparents. In the absence of traditional caregivers, children are left at a nursery school or daycare center during the day. Children are expected to be obedient and respectful toward elders and to help with household chores, tending livestock, or minding younger siblings.

THE ROLE OF WOMEN

When discussing the role of Vietnamese women, it is impossible to ignore the daring feat of the Trung sisters and their band of 20 women warriors, who staged the first important rebellion against the Chinese between A.D. 40 and A.D. 43. Although the sisters were eventually defeated, the story of their brave act has survived almost 2,000 years of history, inspiring the Vietnamese in times of oppression.

Their defeat signaled not only the beginning of a long period of Chinese political domination but also the imposition of Confucian thought on Vietnamese society. Women were thereafter expected to play a subservient role. According to Confucianism, as a daughter, a woman must obey her father; as a wife, her husband; and as a widow, her son. In addition, women were to cultivate the Four Virtues—gentleness in speech, pleasantness in appearance, demureness in behavior, and skill in homemaking.

By and large, this perception of women was retained until the 20th century, but in reality, the Confucian ideal of women remaining at home was never rigidly observed in Vietnam. In the villages, for example, peasant women sometimes ran their own businesses or traveled to other villages to trade on market days. Female poets, writers, teachers, and political figures have appeared through the centuries, the most famous being Ho Xuan Huong, an outspoken poet in the 19th century. Vietnam is thought to have once been a matriarchial society.

Women have always been active in the buying and selling of food in markets.

CHANGES IN PERCEPTION The call to recognize equality for women began in the same period as the movement for nationalism. The 1920s and 1930s saw the publication of many women's periodicals and the formation of the first modern women's organizations. One of these was the Women's Labor Study Association, started by Nguyen Khoa Tung, better known by her pen name, Dam Phuong. Dam Phuong took a practical approach to the goal of equality for women, believing that the first step was to equip women with education and skills.

From 1929 to 1934 Nguyen Duc Nhuan published *Phu Nu Tan Van*, a women's newspaper. It printed contributions from many women writers, among them Nguyen Thi Khiem (alias Manh Manh), Nguyen Thi Chinh, Phan Thi Bach Van, and Van Dai.

In the 1930s, the Bicycle Movement got under way. Supporters of this movement were young women from the middle class who toured Vietnam on bicycles instead of spending their time at home.

The collective aim of these early women's associations was to obtain equal rights and recognition. For instance, they advocated free marriage with the partner of one's choice rather than traditional arranged marriage; getting equal pay for equal work; and eliminating double standards for chastity and fidelity.

There is a Vietnamese Women's Musuem in Hanoi, which is dedicated to recognizing the varied and imporant contributions that Vietnamese women have made.

Vietnamese women are becoming increasingly independent. Many now run their own businesses.

Daycare centers meet an increasing demand from working women.

IDEALS The women wanted to see an end to gender segregation, wife-beating, and outdated Confucian values concerning women. They also shared with the nationalists the desire for universal suffrage, which at that time had not been legislated.

After North Vietnam declared its independence in 1945, Vietnamese women achieved a number of goals. In 1946, 10 women were elected to the first National Assembly and the Vietnam Women's Union was formed from the earlier Women's Association.

In 1959 the Law on Marriage and the Family was passed by the National Assembly. This law did away with the old customs of arranged marriage, polygamy, concubinage, and the father's automatic custody of children in cases of divorce. The law also ensured better working conditions, maternity leave, free childcare and universal suffrage.

Today, Vietnamese women are represented in the middle ranks of government, in the people's committees, in trade unions, in cooperatives, and in military organizations.

They enjoy better educational opportunities, and many have full-time careers. Many women joined the army and led dangerous missions both in the north and in the south during the war.

And still, as a leader of the Vietnam Women's Union has described it, "We have equality but we are not yet equal."

Like women in other parts of the world, modern Vietnamese women face a dilemma: they are expected to succeed in the workplace while maintaining their full-time role at home as wives and mothers.

LIFE CYCLE

In Vietnam the significant events in life—birth, marriage, and death—were once marked by elaborate ceremonies. During and after the war years, they became simpler out of necessity and because of the austere communist ideology. In the past decade or so, there has been a return to more elaborate, traditional rituals, especially for weddings and funerals.

"Girl or boy" is not as much of an issue for these children as it was for their parents.

BIRTH AND CHILDHOOD Children are the cherished goal of Vietnamese marriages, and the birth of a child is a joyous occasion. The Vietnamese family is likely to have a small party when the baby is one month old. When infant mortality was high, the family concealed their joy to prevent jealous spirits from harming the baby. Often a child was not given a proper name for a few years, and in the meantime a nickname was used to fool the evil spirits.

In the past, boys were preferred. An old Vietnamese saying goes, "A single boy, that is positive; 10 girls, that is still negative!" These days, girls are loved as much as boys, but they are also given greater responsibility at home and less freedom to roam. Boys—particularly the eldest—grow up understanding that the future care of their parents and unmarried sisters will be their responsibility as soon as they are old enough to assume it.

MARRIAGE In the past, parents enlisted the help of matchmakers to choose appropriate marriage partners for their children. Fortune-tellers were also consulted to see if the couples' horoscopes were compatible and to choose auspicious days for ceremonies. Ceremonies for the proposal and the engagement took place one or two years before the wedding. These traditions have loosened somewhat but are still widely observed.

The wedding ceremony consists of two parts. During the first part the groom, with his parents and a small group of family members or friends, goes to the bride's home to seek her parents' permission to marry her. Often, the groom presents the traditional offering of betel leaves and areca nuts to the bride's family. After the groom has made a formal proposal, the bride's family consults the ancestors at the family altar.

A groom fetches his bride from her family home. Young Vietnamese are rediscovering traditional dress for special events.

For the second part, there is a celebration after the bride and groom have performed certain rituals at an altar erected for the occasion. Traditionally, at this ceremony held at the groom's house, the god of marriage, the Old Man in the Moon, is asked to bless and protect the couple. Three tiny cups are filled with rice wine. The elder who leads the ceremony bows before the altar, takes a sip from one of the cups, and passes it to the groom. The groom takes a sip and then passes the cup to the bride, who does likewise. The groom then takes a piece of ginger and rubs it in salt, and both bride and groom eat it to signify their lasting love. Only then are they ready to exchange wedding rings.

Once the solemnities are over, it is time for a feast with family and friends. If the couple can afford it, the wedding feast is held at a restaurant, and a wedding car is hired for the occasion to transport the newly married couple to their destination. Many Vietnamese couples in the cities wear both the traditional dress and Western wedding attire (a bridal gown for the woman and a suit for the man) at different moments during the wedding festivities.

In the past, the groom had to give a dowry before he was permitted to marry a woman. This practice is not formally observed today, but men are still expected to give jewelry and other gifts to the bride and her family.

DEATH Funerals are elaborate affairs, expressing respect and care for the deceased, who are thought to reciprocate with care for their living descendants.

To ensure a comfortable afterlife, the family provides colorful model paper houses, spirit money, and other necessities that are burned, enabling the departed soul to use them.

During the wake, relatives take turns guarding the coffin at night. Previously, a coin was placed in the mouth of the deceased for luck and a bowl of rice was left on the coffin. In some parts of Vietnam, a knife is placed on the stomach to ward off evil spirits before the body is buried.

Of all of life's events, the most elaborate preparations are reserved for funerals. Mutual aid societies help family members with the heavy funeral expenses.

THE FUNERAL For the funeral procession, clothes of sackcloth or gauze are worn by family members. After the burial, the family goes through a period of mourning that can last anywhere from nine months to more than three years. More traditional Vietnamese wear a mourning band on their sleeve during this time and refrain from going to parties or indulging in other entertainment.

Exhumation is commonly practiced in Vietnam. Three years after the burial, family members exhume the body from the gravesite and collect the bones of the deceased. The bones are cleaned and placed in a smaller earthen coffin for reburial.

The dead are not forgotten. A photograph is usually placed on the family altar at home and sometimes also in a temple. Offerings in the form of food or incense are made to the spirit of the deceased on special occasions and on the anniversary of the death.

LIVING IN THE CITY

One in every five Vietnamese lives in an urban area. Ho Chi Minh City is the largest of these areas, with a population of 6 million. The capital, Hanoi, is the next largest. Other major cities are Haiphong, Da Nang, Nha Trang, Quy Nhon, and Hue.

Most people prefer to live near their workplace. The shophouses or low-rise apartment buildings where they live may have two or three rooms, a small kitchen, and a bathroom. There may also be a small courtyard for drying laundry. Apartments on the upper floors usually have a balcony or roof garden. Most of the large colonial houses built by the French have

City markets offer a fascinating variety of stalls.

70

been converted into offices or subdivided into apartments.

The city comes alive when the sun comes up. As early as 6 A.M., trucks and buses rumble on their way to the provinces, honking at smaller vehicles to clear the path. By 6:30 in the morning, the city's main streets are filled with columns of people on bicycles and scooters weaving their way to work. Hawkers selling noodle soup, French bread, or *xoi* (soy), a kind of sticky rice, park their pushcarts on sidewalks and workers eat breakfast at these stalls. In the marketplace, housewives buy fresh vegetables, fish, and pork or chicken for the day's meals.

Most offices close at 4 P.M., but shops in Hanoi and Ho Chi Minh City remain open until 8 or 9 P.M. On their way home, workers enjoy browsing through the shops or stopping at a café for a drink. Some stop at the market to buy food for dinner.

In the evening, many adults attend courses at community centers or work at a second job to supplement their income.

The city bustle and rush is felt even by schoolgirls who know the advantage of having wheels to get around quickly.

When pumps are not available, traditional irrigation methods are used to transfer water from one rice field to another. Village life is far from relaxed. Farmers toil for long hours in the sun, and even attend agricultural institutes to keep up with the latest developments.

VILLAGE LIFE

Before television was introduced, the status symbol of a village household was a chiming clock. But village life is not so much determined by the minute and the hour as by the seasons. Fields have to be plowed and harrowed and rice must be sown twice a year during the dry seasons. Seedlings are transplanted only after the first rains. The seasons dictate when the grain will ripen and be harvested.

Farmers have increased their output of grain, fruit, vegetables, and livestock because they are permitted to sell their produce on the free market.

People are organized into teams, young men taking on heavy tasks such as plowing and digging canals, women helping in the backbreaking work of transplanting rice seedlings. Older folk are assigned to look after fruit trees or to tend pond fish. Grain storage, construction of buildings, and fertilizing are assigned to a team of villagers.

Villages in the northern and central regions consist of several hamlets surrounded by a protective bamboo hedge. The village entrance is usually marked by a wooden or brick gate with the name of the village displayed on it. Villages in the south are more informal and houses tend to be built along a main road or canal rather than around a village square.

Larger villages have a cinema, a hairdressing salon, and a few small cafés and general stores.

Houses are traditionally built of wood or bamboo with thatch roofs. Richer villagers have rebuilt their houses in brick with tiled roofs and glass window panes. There is no central heating during the cool winter months, so houses in the north tend to be compact. Southern houses are more spacious and have larger windows for ventilation because of the relatively warm weather there.

Modern toilets are not widely available. Cities are well served by electricity, but some villages are still out of the power grids' reach. The government plans to build more power plants. In 2003, 44 percent of electricity was still provided by fossil fuels.

Sunset signals the time to rest and be with the family.

RELIGION

MORE THAN HALF OF VIETNAMESE are Buddhists, while the rest are Christians, Muslims, Hindus, or members of syncretic sects such as the Cao Dai and Hoa Hao. Beliefs from animism, Taoism, and Confucianism have been integrated into much of Vietnamese religious practice.

RELIGION AND THE STATE

The Vietnamese Constitution provides for freedom of worship. A person has freedom of religious activity as long as such activity does not violate the laws of the state, hamper productive work, or jeopardize the security of the country. Fortune-telling, such as palm reading, astrology, and geomancy, are considered superstitions. Although discouraged by the government, they are still practiced by some Vietnamese.

"Our karma we must carry as our lot. Let's stop decrying Heaven's whims and quirks. Inside ourselves there lies the root of good: the heart outweighs all talents on this earth."

—from *The Tale of Kieu* by Nguyen Du (1765–1820)

Left: **A small Muslim community lives in Ho Chi Minh City.**

Opposite: **A lady offers her prayers in a temple on New Year's Day.**

A monk in Ha Tien, in southern Vietnam.

BUDDHISM

Buddhism is the religion of the majority of Vietnamese. Hanoi was a center for Vietnamese Buddhism as early as the second century A.D. In the past, many joined the Buddhist priesthood for reasons other than religious salvation. For some, it was the only way to get an education and socially upgrade themselves. For others, it was an escape from taxation and military service.

By commissioning temples to be built in every village, the kings remained closely linked to Buddhism and used it to reach the people. Although Theravada Buddhism is practiced in Vietnam, Mahayana Buddhism is predominant. One difference between the two is the concept of bodhisattva in Mahayana Buddhism. A bodhisattva is someone who has attained enlightenment but in compassion stays behind to help his fellow men toward the same goal. Historically, one of the ways to help others was to advise the king in political affairs, which is how Buddhist monks gained political influence. Their role, however, considerably diminished after the 13th century with the growing influence of Confucianism.

Buddhist monks also played a role in Vietnamese politics in the 1960s when the South Vietnamese, who were mainly Buddhists and were

BUDDHIST BELIEFS

Buddhism originated in India in 534 B.C. Its teachings were spread by the disciples of Prince Siddhartha Gautama. He was later called Buddha, which means the awakened one.

The aim of Buddhism is to reach a rational analysis of life and its problems, and Buddha sought to solve this puzzle by formulating the Eightfold Path and the Four Noble Truths. The Four Noble Truths are that humans are born to suffer from one life to another; humans crave pleasure, possessions, and the cessation of pain, and this craving causes suffering; the cure for craving is non-attachment to all things including the self; and to achieve nonattachment, one must take the Eightfold Path to righteousness—right conduct, effort, intention, livelihood, meditation, mindfulness, speech, and views.

Buddhists believe that karma, or cause and effect, determines one's destiny. Humans go through a cycle of rebirth, and the next life could be one of suffering or of ease depending on one's karma. The process of rebirth continues until a state of enlightenment is reached.

According to Mahayana Buddhism, the form of the religion that reached Vietnam through China, one who has reached nirvana may choose to remain in this world to help others and lead them to enlightenment.

dissatisfied with the Diem government, alleged that its policies favored the Catholic population. When crowds of Buddhists took to the streets to celebrate Buddha's birthday on May 8, 1963, government troops opened fire and killed nine people. On June 11, 1963, a Buddhist monk set himself on fire in Saigon in public protest. A few other monks did the same in the following months. These and similar incidents were used by Buddhists to attract the world's attention to the tyranny of the Diem government.

CONFUCIANISM

Confucianism was introduced to Vietnam over 2,000 years ago. Although often thought to be a religion, it is in fact a philosophy. Confucius was a teacher and philosopher who lived in China during the period of the Warring States.

He formulated a code of ethics that prescribed the correct conduct for all citizens of a state. The emperor had the heaviest responsibility, and the well-being of the people depended on his behavior. Confucius believed that if an emperor ruled justly and wisely, and was free from personal corruption, the affairs of state would proceed smoothly.

Ancestor worship is an important ritual of Confucianism. Offerings are made to the souls of ancestors on the anniversary of the death as well as during many festivals.

CITIZENS' CODE In Confucianism, the citizen was also expected to develop certain qualities: *nhan* (ny-uhn)—to treat others with mercy and kindness; *le* (lay)—to respect the hierarchies of family and society, and perform rites to maintain family and social order; *nghia* (ngee-AH)—to help the needy; *tri* (tree)—to use wisdom to distinguish good and evil; and *tin* (tin)—to be loyal and trustworthy. Confucius hoped to create, through this code of ethics, a society in which a sense of morality would guide people to behave correctly.

TAM GIAO

Many Vietnamese combine Buddhist beliefs with aspects of ancestor worship found in Confucianism and aspects of deity worship found in Taoism. Vietnamese scholars call this practice Tam Giao or the Triple Religion. Unlike religions such as Islam and Christianity, Buddhism, Confucianism, and Taoism are open to the idea of fusions with other beliefs. Mahayana Buddhism accepts the existence of more than one Buddha; Taoism is based on the tradition of noninterference and incorporates the worship of many gods, including patron saints and the spirits of famous generals; and Confucianism respects all forms of learning and advocates the worship of ancestors.

On the altar of a typical Vietnamese temple one may find among several images those of Buddha, Quan Am (the Goddess of Mercy), and Ngoc Hoang (the Taoist Jade Emperor or God of Heaven). Worshipers may decide to pray and make offerings of incense to one or all of the deities.

ANIMISM

In Vietnam some aspects of animism, a belief in the spiritual nature of living and nonliving things, have also been incorporated into established religion. Five thousand years ago, the Viets believed the world was populated by gods and spirits, some benevolent, others evil. These spirits were everywhere. A tree, a mountain, or a river might have a spirit or a number of spirits residing in it.

One had to be careful not to mention a spirit by name; this could result in harm to the speaker. Dangerous animals such as tigers, elephants, and crocodiles also had spirits, so when referring to them, one did not use their names but called them lord as a show of respect.

CATHOLICISM

Catholicism was brought to Vietnam in the 16th and 17th centuries by Portuguese, French, and Spanish missionaries. Vietnam's Catholic popu-

St. Joseph's Cathedral in Hanoi was built by the French during the colonial years.

lation of 8 million makes it the second largest in Asia after the Philippines. Catholic churches are found throughout Vietnam, although at the time of the Vietminh takeover of North Vietnam in 1954, 700,000 Catholics, fearing religious persecution, fled to the south. During the 1970s, land seized from the Catholic churches was gradually returned to them.

79

Cao Dai services are held four times daily: at six in the morning and evening, at noon, and at midnight.

CAO DAI AND HOA HAO SECTS

Two Buddhist sects—the Cao Dai, founded in 1926, and the Hoa Hao, founded in 1939—were at their most active during Vietnam's period of nationalist struggle. In the 1940s and 1950s, until their repression by President Ngo Dinh Diem, the Hoa Hao were the most powerful military force in the Mekong delta. The Cao Dai were also active resistance fighters who supported the Japanese in the 1940s and aimed to drive out the French colonists.

The Hoa Hao sect has been described as reformed Buddhism based on personal faith rather than elaborate ritual. There are an estimated 3 to 4 million followers of this sect.

The Cao Dai sect was founded by Ngo Minh Chieu. He sought to create the ideal religion by fusing Buddhism with Christianity and elements of Taoism and Confucianism. Cao Dai is actually the name given to the Supreme Being, who is represented by the symbol of the divine eye as revealed in a vision to its founder.

Followers of Cao Dai are vegetarians and practice celibacy. They seek divine truth through the spirits of famous nationalists, writers, and other eminent people. Spirits of personalities who have inspired them include Victor Hugo, Louis Pasteur, Joan of Arc, Dr. Sun Yat Sen, Vladimir Lenin, Confucius, and William Shakespeare. The sect has 7 to 8 million members.

BUDDHIST-CHRISTIAN BELIEFS

Tinh Do Cu Si is a minority sect that combines Buddhist and Christian beliefs. It was founded in 1945 by Nguyen Thanh Nam, nicknamed the Coconut Monk because he is believed to have lived only on coconuts for three years. His hope was to reunify Vietnam peacefully. He led a small band of followers on Phung Island in the 1940s. He was imprisoned several times for opposing the policies of the Diem government.

A memorial to the Coconut Monk.

VESTON
NHẬN MAY
ART
châu
CHÂN DUNG
QUẢNG CÁO
HỘP ĐÈN · CHỮ NỔI
UỐN
403
SẮT
XÂY DỰNG
Ø6 :
Ø8 :
Ø10 :
Ø12 :
Ø14 :
Ø16 :

LANGUAGE

VIETNAMESE IS THE OFFICIAL LANGUAGE of the country. A language of mixed origins, Vietnamese traces its roots to the dialects used by the first settlers of the Red River civilization—the Mon-Khmers, the Tai, and the Southern Chinese. Linguists suspect that Vietnamese may also be related to Malay and the Polynesian dialects.

Most of its basic vocabulary originates from Tai and Mon-Khmer words, but after the Chinese conquest in the first century, the language gradually developed many similarities to Chinese. This was because many words were adopted from the Chinese, although the Vietnamese pronounced them according to their own speech habits.

Vietnamese is spoken by the ethnic Vietnamese and Chinese who make up the majority in the country. The hill people, the ethnic minorities, have their own numerous dialects, nearly 60 in all, which can be categorized under four linguistic groups.

Romanized VN script

Left: Besides Vietnamese, at least 54 dialects are used by the ethnic minorities in Vietnam.

Opposite: **Quoc ngu**, or romanized Vietnamese script, was developed in the 17th century but only widely used in the 20th century.

ETHNIC DIALECTS Linguistic groups for the ethnic dialects can be basically classified as Cham or Malayo-Polynesian; Sino-Tibetan, such as the Meo and Giay dialects; Mon-Khmer dialects, closely related to the Cambodian language and spoken by the Katu, Sedang, and Bahnar; and Tai-Kadai, which is also known as Thay or Thai and is spoken (with dialectal variations) by the Tai subgroups, the Black, Red, and White Tai.

SAME WORD, DIFFERENT MEANING

Vietnamese is a tonal, monosyllabic language. Each word is expressed by a single syllable, and each syllable is pronounced in one of six tones, which are: high rising, low falling, low rising, high broken, low broken and flat (no tone). Foreigners trying to learn Vietnamese often find the tonal differences more complicated than those of Mandarin, or other Chinese dialects that have only four tones. The tones are indicated with a tone symbol above the syllable and determines the word's meaning. For example, *ca* with a flat tone means sing, but means fish when said with a high rising tone. The most common example of tonal differences is the word *ma*. Depending on how the syllable is pronounced, *ma* can mean cheek, horse, tomb, ghost, but, or rice seedling. In a culture that stresses the importance of correct forms of address, using the incorrect tone may be something of a social disaster.

Romanized VN script

A man uses *quoc ngu*, or romanized Vietnamese, to write on signboards.

*[handwritten notes: * chủ nho = chinese characters * chủ Nôm — * Romanized VN]*

WRITTEN LANGUAGE

Before the 13th century, the Vietnamese imperial court used an ideographic form of writing that was based on Chinese characters known as *chu nho* (chur-nyawh). Gradually, the scholars and ruling elite developed a system that also used Chinese characters but relied more on phonetics than ideographs. This modified system was known as *chu nom* (chur-noam) or, more simply, *nom*.

Nom was the language of the scholars. Provincial and national examinations were conducted in *nom*. Imperial edicts, history and geography books, novels and poems were recorded using this system of modified Chinese characters. Even after the introduction of *quoc ngu* (romanized Vietnamese) many Vietnamese poets and scholars in the 18th and 19th centuries continued to use *chu nom*, and some of Vietnam's best known works were first written in *nom*, to be popularized later in *quoc ngu*. Until the early 20th century, *chu nom* was regarded as the official written form of Vietnamese and *quoc ngu* was relegated to more mundane use.

Whether the Vietnamese had their own system of writing before the Chinese system was adopted is uncertain. Ethnologists note that the Tay of the northern hills have a form of writing similar to that used by lowland Vietnamese until the 16th century.

Buddhists at an evening class use books written in *quoc ngu*. A great number of books first written in *chu nom* have been translated into *quoc ngu*.

A 16th-century Japanese covered bridge in Hoi An, the port where the first Portuguese missionaries landed in Vietnam.

"One characteristic of newly independent Vietnam was the barefooted peasant walking to evening classes, tiny oil lamp in one hand, battered quoc ngu *primer in the other."*

—David Marr,
Vietnamese Tradition on Trial 1920–45

QUOC NGU

In 1614, the Portuguese established the first Catholic mission at Hoi An in central Vietnam. They were soon joined by Spanish and French missionaries. One of these was the French Jesuit priest Alexandre de Rhodes. A brilliant scholar and linguist, he is said to have mastered Vietnamese and preached in the language only six months after his arrival.

To make the gospel available to the Vietnamese, de Rhodes devised the phonetic romanized script known as *quoc ngu*. It became the accepted script. The first *quoc ngu*-Portuguese-Latin dictionary was published in 1651, and missionaries were able to translate prayer books and catechisms into Vietnamese. In the late 19th century, *quoc ngu* was introduced to schools in the south. The north, which had stronger scholastic traditions, continued using *chu nom*.

In 1908 the royal court in Hue directed the education ministry to start a new curriculum based entirely on *quoc ngu*. Later, with the onset of World War I, there was an urgent need for the French and Vietnamese to learn a common language—the French were shorthanded and needed to train Vietnamese as junior officials in the colonial administration. They also hoped that by popularizing *quoc ngu*, they would be able to establish a friendly dialogue between French officials and the Vietnamese. The French hoped to discourage the Vietnamese from picking up dangerous ideas about nationalism and independence, the topics of intellectual discussion in Europe at the time. The French plan backfired.

In the 1920s and 1930s there was a sudden flowering of *quoc ngu*. Newspapers, periodicals, and pamphlets appeared all over Vietnam in which scholars and intellectuals argued passionately for and against nationalism, free marriage (as opposed to arranged marriage), and a wide variety of other topics. The popularization of *quoc ngu* meant that many peasants and shopkeepers were able to read the criticism of national issues and then discuss them with their less literate neighbors. Many of these publications were censored by the French and eventually banned, but the Vietnamese appetite for literacy and nationalism had been whetted.

Children outside their village school in a Haiphong suburb.

Nevertheless, it was only after World War II that literacy in *quoc ngu* spread down to the poorest people. Although the enthusiasm for reading was evident in the earlier part of the 20th century, most Vietnamese were peasants who could just afford basic necessities such as food and clothing; paying school fees for their children was out of the question. But after 1945 the Vietminh began a widespread program of compulsory free education for children and basic education for adults. This made it possible to discuss their ideas and goals for nationalism and also proved extremely useful later in organizing the struggle for independence.

READING AND PRONOUNCING QUOC NGU   The majority of Vietnamese are able to read *quoc ngu*, the result of the intensive post-World War II literacy program.

Quoc ngu consists of 12 vowels and 27 consonants. Accent marks are used to indicate vowel changes and tones. Most of the consonants are pronounced as they would be in English. Exceptions include: *d* without the crossbar sounds like *z* in the north and *y* in the south; *gi* is pronounced *zee* in the north and *yee* in the south, while *tr* is pronounced as *ch*.

Although Vietnamese is spoken throughout the country, northerners pronounce certain words differently from southerners. Generally, northern pronunciation has harder, more clearly defined consonants. People in the south lengthen their vowels so that their words have a softer sound. Even the provinces have their own distinctive pronunciations. People from different regions sometimes have difficulty understanding each other.

The few English words on city signs are intended to help foreign customers.

A SECOND LANGUAGE

Many Vietnamese speak a second language. French is not as widely used as is commonly assumed, since only the Vietnamese elite had the benefit of a French education and the lower classes did not mix with upper-class Vietnamese or with the French. In high school, many students choose to learn English. French, Mandarin, and Japanese are the other choices. Russian is less widely used now.

BORROWED WORDS

Several Chinese words have found their way into the Vietnamese vocabulary. For example, the Vietnamese words for north, south, east, and west are *bac* (bahk), *nam* (nahm), *dong* (doang), and *tay* (tai) from the Chinese *bei, nan, dong,* and *xi.* Tea in Vietnamese is *tra* (chra), from the Chinese *cha.* Words of French origin also appear in Vietnamese. Soap is *xa bong* (*savon*), coffee is *ca phe* (*café*), and cheese is *pho mat* (*fromage*).

NAMES

There are about 300 family or clan names, but those most commonly found are Le, Pham, Tran, Ngo, Vu, Do, Dao, Duong, Dang, Dinh, Hoang, and Nguyen, the last being the Smith of Vietnam, as it is the family name of almost half of Vietnamese.

Vietnamese place the family name first, followed by a middle name, and the given name is last. The middle name is often used to indicate the generation of the person. Each clan or family has a list of middle names, using a different one for each generation. Brothers of the family Nguyen are likely to have the same middle name, for example, Nguyen *Van* Nhac, Nguyen *Van* Lu, and Nguyen *Van* Hue. They would be addressed by their given names, that is, Mr. Nhac, Mr. Lu, and Mr. Hue.

Vietnamese like to give their daughters names that embody beauty and femininity, such as Hoa, which means flower.

NAME-GIVING It is common to name girls after rivers, birds, flowers, or precious things. Popular names for girls are Phuong (phoenix), Cuc (chrysanthemum), and Hoa (flower). Boys are usually given an abstract name that denotes a personal quality such as Duc (virtue) or Khiem (modesty). Roman Catholic Vietnamese have Christian names.

A Vietnamese woman often keeps her maiden name after marriage but may use her husband's given name to introduce herself to others. So if Miss Le Thi Lam marries Mr. Do Van Tien, she would call herself Mrs. Tien. But at work she would be known as Mrs. Le Thi Lam.

FORMS OF ADDRESS

In Vietnamese society, respect is given to those older than oneself. This stems from the deeply embedded teachings of Confucius that place emphasis on one's rank and position in society and the respect that goes

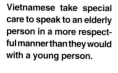

Vietnamese take special care to speak to an elderly person in a more respectful manner than they would with a young person.

with each position. Thus, a grandmother would command the respect of her daughter and her grandchildren.

A younger person addresses an older man by the term *ong* (awng), and an older woman by the term *ba* (bah). A man or woman of the same age would be addressed by *anh* (aenh) and *co* (ko) respectively. Close friends, relatives, or younger persons may be addressed by *em* (em); this term is also used by men to address their sweethearts.

Bac (bahk) is a respectful term not restricted to relatives. The most obvious example is Bac (Uncle) Ho, a term of respect for President Ho Chi Minh. Forms of address can be used to establish respect or social distance. If a young person addresses a much older one with *ong* instead of *bac*, for example, the older man may sense a coolness or even disrespect.

Chao *is a typical Vietnamese greeting. It can mean good morning, good day, good evening, and even goodbye.*

THE LEGEND OF UNCLE TOAD

One day toad and his animal friends decided to journey to Heaven to appeal to the Jade Emperor for rain during an extremely long drought.

The Jade Emperor was furious that a mere toad had dared to enter his celestial palace and ordered his guards to chase the group away. But the bees stung the guards, and the other animals created an uproar, and no one could catch the hopping toad. Impressed by the animals' determination, the emperor granted the toad an audience and soon found out what was troubling the earth. He promised to deliver rain and, out of respect, called the toad uncle. He also forbade the animals to make such a long and dangerous journey in future. If ever there was another drought, all Uncle Toad had to do was to call out loudly, and the emperor would answer his call.

This is how Uncle Toad got his name, and it is also why toads, to this day, call out loudly to bring the rain. "The toad is Heaven's uncle" is a popular Vietnamese saying derived from this legend.

ARTS

THE VIETNAMESE ENJOY A RICH and varied tradition in the arts. Their heritage includes sculpture, music, and dance from the Indianized kingdoms of Funan and Champa in the south and the influence of Chinese culture and Buddhism on almost all forms of the arts in the north.

Some art forms have remained unchanged for centuries. These include traditional theater, or *hat tuong* (hut tw-uhng) and *hat cheo* (hut CHEH-oh), the folk songs known as *hat a dao* (hut-ah-dao), and the dances of the various hill peoples. Prose and poetry went through vigorous changes in style and subject matter through the ages. New forms of musical drama, or *cai luong* (KAI-lung), and spoken drama, or *kich noi* (kik-NOY), have appeared, while during the war years, from the 1950s to the 1970s, music, literature, and drama took on a very patriotic and often martial aspect.

MUSIC

The earliest musical instruments discovered in Vietnam are a large bronze drum and a lithophone. The lithophone resembles a giant xylophone with keys made of stone, the largest measuring about 3.5 feet (1 m) in length. Sound is produced by striking the keys with a mallet. The bronze drum, estimated to be about 3,000 years old, is engraved with figures of dancers, some of them depicted with a *khen* (khen), a mouth organ made from reeds. Over the centuries, the lithophone evolved into the *to rung* (toe RUHNG), a bamboo xylophone that produces ringing yet fluid notes. The bronze drum spawned a whole percussion set, including skin drums, gongs, and cymbals. Percussion instruments set the tone or mood for each scene in traditional drama.

Opposite: **A wood sculptor works on a carving of a large Buddha statue.**

Below: **Children from the School of the Blind learning traditional music.**

Percussion instruments provide the rhythm and set the mood of festival and religious ceremonies.

OTHER INSTRUMENTS Wind instruments, such as the bamboo flute and Chinese oboe, and string instruments also form part of the Vietnamese orchestra. Some string instruments—such as the lute, zither, and a two-stringed violin that looks like a long, large pipe—are Chinese in origin.

Others, like the *dan bau* (dahn bow), or monochord (one-stringed guitar), are typically Vietnamese. The *dan bau* is made from a dried calabash or gourd to which a curved stick has been attached. A single copper wire is stretched across the gourd and along the length of the stick. To play the *dan bau* a musician has to pluck the copper wire with a pick, while his other hand moves the flexible, curved stick. This varies the pitch.

Another typically Vietnamese instrument is the *vo de cam* (vaw duh cam), a long-handled guitar with three strings. The sound box is different from other string instruments, being rectangular and open at the bottom.

The *dan nguyet* (dahn noo-yet) is a two-stringed, moon-shaped lute that has prominently raised frets along its narrow, long neck. It is an important instrument in chamber music and is used to accompany other musical and theatrical performances.

SONGS THROUGH THE CENTURIES

Since the 11th-century Ly dynasty, a wide repertoire of popular music has developed. In addition, the numerous ethnic groups in Vietnam have given rise to a wide range of musical styles.

From the provinces, *hat a dao*, a performance of poetic songs, became very popular, and many of these songs were written down and passed on to the next generation. At the other extreme are the *trong quan* (choang kwuhn) or *quan ho* (kwuhn ho). These are a part of spring festivals. The songs are often extemporaneous; a group of boys sing one verse, then the girls improvise a verse in reply.

The songs of the boatwomen who plied their vessels across the Perfume River west of Hue also became popular. Many songs recount the heroic exploits of Vietnamese warriors or relate popular legends.

At the court in Hanoi, and later in Hue, a different sort of music developed. There were three categories: *dai nhac* (dai nyahk) or great music, chamber music for the entertainment of the king, and ritual music accompanying important ceremonies such as the one to ensure a good harvest.

The Ly kings, in particular Ly Thai To and Ly Cao To, were especially fond of Cham music. They brought back captives who had been performers in the court of Champa. In this way, Cham ballet and the typically plaintive Cham music influenced the Vietnamese performing arts.

Quan ho singers.

The ageless themes of Vietnamese opera offer hours of entertainment.

THE THEATER

With the exception of the modern spoken drama called *kich noi*, Vietnamese drama is inseparably linked to music and dance. *Cai luong,* literally renovated theater, may be compared to a Western operetta or musical. It includes songs, dances, and recitations. Themes can be historical or modern (urban or rural); one popular theme is the life of Emperor Gia Long.

In traditional theaters—*hat cheo* and *hat tuong*—the audience is familiar with the stage characters, who are expected to keep to the conventional dress, make-up, gestures, and speech of the stock characters. The make-up helps the audience to identify the hero and the heroine, the evil and the good characters. For instance, a red face signifies courage and loyalty, while a white face betrays a traitor or cruel person. Black faces indicate mountain people; lowlanders have green faces. As in Chinese opera, on which *tuong* is based, plots are taken from legends and stories of great warriors, for example, the story of the Trung sisters' rebellion.

But unlike Chinese opera, where female roles are played by male actors, actresses appear in *tuong*.

Cheo is a more lighthearted, often a satirical variation of *tuong*. A stock character, *he cheo* (the buffoon), is usually present, and plots may be drawn from folktales.

Kich noi, or spoken drama, made its appearance in Hanoi in 1921 with Vu Dinh Long's *The Cup of Poison* (*Chen Thuoc Doc*), a comedy about a wastrel who is talked out of committing suicide. Another playwright of that period was Vi Huyen Dac, whose works *Kim Tien* (*Money*) and *Uyen-uong* (*Lovers*) were especially popular.

WATER PUPPETRY

One delightfully entertaining dramatic form that is uniquely Vietnamese is the water-puppet show. Puppet shows, or *roi can* (zoi cahn), were traditionally performed at royal celebrations or as part of Buddhist festivals. Water puppetry, or *roi nuoc* (zoi nw-UHK), is thought to have developed during the 10th century as part of an agricultural ceremony performed during the rainy season.

A modern *kich noi* performance.

The most elaborate shows are staged at pagodas in Ha Son Binh province and around Hanoi. Water-puppet shows are performed outdoors over a small pond. The puppeteers stand waist-deep in water, hidden by bamboo screens or a puppet house, as they cleverly manipulate the rods attached to the puppets. Every performance begins with an introduction by Teu the clown. A single firecracker or a joss stick is then lighted to signal the start of the performance. Plots are often based on legends and folktales, and the watery surface makes an ideal setting for the retelling of stories such as *The Golden Turtle and the Lake of the Restored Sword*.

Opposite: **A girl crouches
at a book stall to read
comic books. About 92
percent of Vietnamese
women are literate.**

LITERATURE

Vietnam's literary field is rich in poetry, prose, verse-novels, and essays, as well as commentaries on history, geography, and medicine. Most of the works produced by writers and poets before the 14th century used the Chinese script *chu nho.* The 14th to the 17th centuries saw an increase in the use of the newly developed *chu nom* by Vietnamese scholars, who wrote volumes of Tang-influenced poetry, novels, and commentaries.

The oldest surviving works date back to the 11th century, when Buddhist philosophy influenced Vietnamese poetry. Some of these were penned by Dieu Nhan, a Buddhist nun who lived from 1042 to 1114, Vietnam's first known woman writer.

During the Ly and Tran dynasties (11th to 15th centuries) there were many eminent scholars and writers, but the figure that dominated this period was Nguyen Trai (1380–1442), a brilliant scholar and military man. He helped a young man named Le Loi to form a resistance group against the Chinese Ming invaders and eventually to establish the Later Le dynasty.

Nguyen Trai wrote extensively on a wide range of subjects, his favorite being geography. But he also composed poetry and prose, the most famous being *Proclamation of Victory Over the Ming*, a prose epic describing, from Le Loi's point of view, the victory over the Ming invaders.

The golden period of classical literature began in the 18th century and stretched into the 19th century. Two eminent women, Doan Thi Diem and Ho Xuan Huong, contributed to the literary scene during this period.

Doan Thi Diem (1705–48) was famous for her *chu nom* translation of the epic poem *The Lament of a Warrior's Wife*, a sensitive and lyrical rewriting of a poem first composed in classical Chinese. A gifted scholar who, being a woman, could not sit for the imperial examinations, she nonetheless coached scholars for those examinations. Her other well-known work is *New Collection of Wonderful Stories*, a compilation of legends from China.

Ho Xuan Huong lived in the late 18th century. She was an intelligent woman who enjoyed the company of other writers and scholars. Her poems are among the most popular even today and noted for their simple language, strong images, and witty double-entendres. They contain many nonconformist ideas, all the more unusual for having been suggested by a woman. In them, pompous officials and arrogant scholars are brought down, while Huong's sympathy for unmarried mothers, belief in equality for women, and advocacy for free love are evident.

Of Vietnam's many great novels, two classics stand out and are widely read even today. One is *Luc Van Tien*, written by the blind poet and scholar Nguyen Dinh Chieu (1822–88). The novel is a moving story that revolves around a young man named Luc, and highlights the importance of fidelity and the sacrifices made for a just cause.

The other is Vietnam's beloved classic *Kim Van Kieu,* or *The Tale of Kieu.* Written by Nguyen Du (1765–1820), *Kieu*, as it is popularly known, is a verse-novel, an epic that runs into 3,254 verses.

THE STORY OF KIEU

In Nguyen Du's ageless love story, Kim meets Kieu, and they fall in love and plan to marry. Then Kieu's father is accused of wrongdoing and imprisoned. To release her father, Kieu agrees to become a concubine to the evil merchant Ma Giam Sinh and tells her younger sister Van to marry Kim instead. Later, Kieu discovers to her horror that Sinh is a pimp and intends to use her for prostitution. At Sinh's brothel, Kieu meets Thuc, a young man who rescues her and takes her as his secret concubine. Thuc's wife gets wind of this and has Kieu kidnapped to serve as a slave in their house. Thuc dares not admit to his wife Kieu's relationship to him.

Kieu's luck changes when she meets and marries the commander Tu Hai. Life runs smoothly for some time until Tu Hai is slain in battle. In despair at having encouraged her husband to trust the enemy, Kieu throws herself into a river. She is rescued by a Buddhist nun who gives her refuge in her pagoda. Kim, who parted from Kieu 15 years before and has given up his search for her, chances upon this very temple, and the old lovers enjoy a bittersweet reunion.

WRITERS OF THE 20TH CENTURY The 20th century saw dramatic changes in the literary scene. Young Vietnamese intellectuals returned from Europe bursting with new ideas of nationalism, democracy, equal rights, and communism. At the same time, *quoc ngu* was being popularized, and this resulted in a flood of newspapers and journals that provided an arena for heated debates about various topics.

New forms of drama, *kich noi* and *cai luong,* were introduced. Poetry and prose were taking on a new down-to-earth writing style with realistic themes. Literary landmarks in the first half of this century include the novella *The Water Melon* and Ngo Tat To's *When the Light Is Out.* Like many other novels of this period, Ngo Tat To's work depicts the hardships of the people and the desperate choices they made. Other novels, such as *Teacher Minh* by Nguyen Cong Hoan, examine the conflicts in a society faced with opposing modern and traditional values. Nhat Linh, in his well-known work *Doan Tuyet* (*Break Off*), broached the same subject. Among the more recently published works, Bao Ninh's novel *The Sorrow of War* is a realistic personal account of the Vietnam War.

With the increased literacy rate, there is also more need for good literature. Many are turning to translations of texts, and some Vietnamese writers are venturing overseas to have their novels translated into other languages, such as English, and marketed abroad.

ARCHITECTURE AND SCULPTURE

Architecture and sculpture in Vietnam took on two distinct styles before the 11th century. At the time when the Chinese were governing the northern region of Vietnam, the two Indianized states of Funan and Champa flourished in the south.

INDIAN INFLUENCE The city of Oc Eo was one of the major trading centers of the Funan empire, which controlled the shipping routes and territories from southern Cambodia to the Malay peninsula from the first to the sixth centuries A.D. The remains at Oc Eo indicate that large palaces and Hindu temples existed, and that the builders laid out granite foundations for their buildings and had a preference for spacious layouts.

The Cham towers are tall, narrow, and windowless. Cham temples and the remains of a few other Cham buildings can be found at a number of sites in the coastal plain between Da Nang (central Vietnam) and Vung Tau in the south.

Thien Hau Temple displays fine sculptural details, a characteristic of Chinese temples. Chinese migrants to Vietnam built temples with elaborate scenes from Chinese legends and folklore.

CHINESE INFLUENCE The long period of domination by China left a lasting influence in the design of temples and palaces, and in the planning of cities in the north. The Chinese influence on Vietnamese architecture can be seen in the decorative and symbolic sculptures and reliefs in the temples and pagodas.

The Vietnamese also acquired the Chinese practice of building their cities according to geomantic principles. In geomancy, every site, mountain, valley, or river is believed to hold a number of forces that can either benefit or harm its inhabitants. Vietnamese builders use the art of geomancy to select propitious locations and determine how to position buildings. Both the imperial cities of Hanoi and Hue were planned in this way to ensure harmony, balance, and prosperity. When Hue was constructed during the Nguyen dynasty, the natural topography was factored into the design. For instance, the citadel faces south toward Ngu Binh Mount, which is used to screen out evil forces.

CRAFTS

Industrialization has reduced the need for traditionally crafted items, but some crafts, such as lacquerware, wood carvings, and silk paintings, remain popular for decorative purposes.

There are two different types of lacquer—varnish and the more durable pumice. Once used for waterproofing boats and utensils, lacquer is now used to coat all kinds of crafts. Lacquered screens, vases, and furniture, often inlaid with mother-of-pearl or eggshell decorations, are particularly popular in Vietnam. Other decorative crafts such as embroidery serve a religious function. Pieces of cloth embroidered with dragons, mythical animals, and other symbols are used as altar cloths, banners, and pennants to honor deities, patron saints, and social superiors.

PRESERVING FOR THE FUTURE

Modernization has changed the younger generation's taste for folk arts and crafts. It has also affected the ethnic minorities who stand to lose their individual cultures as they slowly acquire the habits of the urban Vietnamese. The need to preserve knowledge of folk and classical Vietnamese art forms was recognized in the 1950s, and institutions such as the Music Academy and Dance School in Hanoi and the National School of Music in Ho Chi Minh City were set up, offering various courses in traditional and Western music. The Arts Institute, which was established later, houses the former Institute of Folklore and Musicology. There is also a school of drama, a film school, and an ethnology museum.

Sacred symbols and mythical animals are brought to life with skillful embroidery.

103

LEISURE

THE LEISURELY PACE of life in the old days is long gone. Most Vietnamese work 10 to 12 hours a day, six days a week. After work there may still be night classes to attend or dinner to prepare for the family. People running their own shops or restaurants have even longer working hours, as the shops usually remain open late into the night and on public holidays. The only time everyone can really take a long break is during the week of the Tet (Vietnamese New Year) celebrations.

Despite these busy schedules, people do find time to relax with friends, take the family on a trip, or play games. Travel is popular, including day trips to the beaches at Vung Tau or Nha Trang and, at special times of the year, pilgrimages to the grottos of Huong Tich (Perfume Pagoda) or the pagodas near Hue. In the countryside, traditional pastimes such as pigeon-flying, eel-catching, and buffalo contests are held as part of local festivals, while the city offers diverse entertainment activities.

"To go to the theater, what joy! A swimming contest comes a poor second. A procession? We might go and have a look, And even a burial passes the time if there's nothing better. But to go and listen to the ten commandments— One must have lost all sense and reason."

—19th-century folk song protesting Emperor Minh Mang's commandments to govern the people's behavior

Left: **Most sporting activities are organized for social purposes rather than on a commercial or professional basis.**

Opposite: **A group of men and women enjoy a relaxed dinner outdoors.**

105

LEISURE IN THE CITY

Vietnamese devote much of their leisure time to social activities. Friends get together after work for drinks, a meal, or an evening at a roadside café to play chess or *tam cuc* (tam kook), a card game similar to poker. These games may go on for hours, while the players snack on grilled cuttlefish or boiled shellfish and drink beer. Chess games often attract a crowd of onlookers who may place bets on the players. Tea stalls at street corners offer patrons—usually older men—a puff on a water pipe or a piece of betel and areca to chew. Elsewhere, on traffic islands and sidewalks, children play simple card games, battledore (hitting a shuttlecock with the foot to keep it in the air), or jump rope.

After school, children may learn a craft or take music lessons.

Young people usually meet in groups at ice cream parlors called *café kem* for coffee, cake, or ice cream, but mostly to talk and socialize. Many take music lessons or craft or language courses organized by youth groups or at private schools. Dance lessons are also offered, and community buildings sometimes house a disco that charges a modest entrance fee for the night. Some places feature local pop groups who perform both local and Western hits.

Municipal theaters and concert halls provide music (classical, folk, and popular), drama (*kich noi* and *cai luong*), ballet, and folk dances. These performances may be given by professional troupes or students from drama schools or conservatories. As fond as they are of watching theater, Vietnamese also enjoy performing, and most cooperatives, youth groups, and factories have their own amateur music or drama group.

Unlike the fast music offered by the discos, dance halls decorated with tiny colored lights specialize in female singers of sentimental songs, who draw an older crowd. If one is simply interested in the music, then there are open-air concerts and beer gardens. Beer gardens vary in the sort of entertainment they offer, from taped music to a live band or simply what is on television that evening.

Other popular forms of entertainment include movies from Hong Kong, Taiwan, and Hollywood, and, less often, locally produced movies. Kung fu, swordfighting, and other action movies draw crowds, but so do romantic tearjerkers. Foreign movies are dubbed in Vietnamese.

Two other forms of entertainment have also proved a hit: karaoke lounges and café videos. Karaoke lounges may be found in all the large coastal towns from Hanoi to Ho Chi Minh City, while café videos are even found in the rural areas.

At a café video, as its name suggests, seating is more or less cinema-style, but with tables. Patrons purchase a drink—beer or soda—and enjoy a video movie, chatting with their friends while watching their favorite show. In the cities, café videos are tucked away on little side streets, while in the provinces a café video is often a shed with walls of bamboo matting.

The disco is one place for Vietnamese to unwind after a hard day's work.

A child fishes at the side of a river.

RURAL PASTIMES

Leisure activities in the villages are not as varied as in the cities, although where electricity is available villages have both the *café kem* and café video. Billiard salons are popular in the south and, like the café video, are often housed in bamboo sheds, giving them a rugged outdoors look.

Television is popular, but in villages that still depend on kerosene and oil lamps, traditional pursuits such as smoking water pipes or playing bamboo flutes, chess, and card games help to pass a pleasant evening. Evenings are also spent at cooperative and party meetings, women's unions, or Buddhist Association gatherings.

In the past, people in the rural areas used to organize cockfighting matches. Fighting contests using fish, buffalo, or crickets were also popular. Wealthy people used to indulge in a game called shrimps' nest or *to tom* (toe tam), a card game considered more complex than the Chinese game of mahjong. Most of these practices have slowly disappeared, although one can occasionally find a group of older men trying their luck.

Several other traditional pastimes have been retained, but they are organized only at certain villages at specific times of the year. Many of them coincide with the Tet celebrations.

BALL-HURLING GAME The Tai living in the northwest hold a contest during the Tet festivities in which contestants have to hurl a ball of multicolored threads through a ring on top of a hoop. This challenging game creates lots of laughter and excitement.

RICE-COOKING CONTEST This contest of speed and skill is held in the Thanh Hoa province southwest of Hanoi toward the end of the year. Village girls compete to build a fire with fresh sugarcane strips to cook a pot of rice. The winner is usually the one who is able to keep the fire going and so is first to cook her rice.

People boarding a bus for the provinces loaded with parcels for relatives and friends. Visiting, particularly during festive seasons, is an important leisure activity.

festive seasons
leisure activity

EEL-CATCHING CONTEST This event is held in Vinh Phu province northwest of Hanoi on the sixth day of Tet. Couples sing and dance while trying to catch an eel placed in an earthen jar of water. The first couple to succeed is the winner.

STORYTELLING In the past, storytellers memorized legends, folktales, and popular novels such as *Kieu*. This was a poor man's craft, and storytellers set their hats down on a street corner or in a teahouse and related their tales. Satisfied listeners left money in the hat.

Badminton and other racket sports are very popular with young people in Vietnam.

SPORTS

The favorite sports in Vietnam are soccer, table tennis, volleyball, swimming, and tennis. In the 22nd SEA Games in 2003, Vietnam beat other Southeast Asian countries to top the scoreboard and finish with 346 medals.

The state encourages sports as a means of keeping fit and provides facilities at community centers and youth clubs. Young people, especially boys, practice various forms of martial arts, including taek won do, judo, karate, and kung fu. To a lesser extent, some learn *vo viet nam* (vaw viet nam), a local form of martial arts that uses bamboo sticks and other weapons as well as the player's bare hands. In school, physical education is part of the curriculum. Older Vietnamese often form groups and meet in the park in the early morning for tai chi or other exercises.

RADIO AND TELEVISION

The national radio station, Voice of Vietnam, began transmission in 1945 and provided information, entertainment, and even companionship during the long war years.

When television first appeared in Vietnam in 1970, people visited neighbors lucky enough to own a set. Now, in many villages, television antennas sit proudly on the thatched roofs of bamboo huts. In the city, 4-foot (1.2 m) satellite-dish antennas sit on rooftops. Television offers a mixture of news, documentaries, locally produced drama serials, and movies from around the world dubbed in Vietnamese.

QUALITY TIME

Vietnamese spend a great deal of their leisure time with their family. As a special treat, parents may take their children by bus or the three-wheeled motor van to the seaside, the beaches at Nha Trang and Vung Tau being the most popular. On Sundays, families may visit the city zoo, botanical gardens, or amusement park. Some Vietnamese simply enjoy a good meal at a street stall or spend time reading in the park.

Since the country's economy has begun to improve, shopping and window-shopping have also become a pastime, while the number of customers browsing in bookstores testifies to the Vietnamese people's lasting love affair with books.

Vietnamese children, like children everywhere, enjoy taking rides in amusement parks.

111

FESTIVALS

FOR THE VIETNAMESE, festivals are more than just fun. They are a binding force and the reason for unity among the people.

Vietnam's major festivals are the Lunar New Year and the Mid-Autumn festival. Festivals to remember the souls of the departed, dates to commemorate heroic events, and important Buddhist anniversaries are also observed throughout the country.

There are also some local festivals that take place only in certain provinces to commemorate a local hero or patron saint.

Roman Catholics celebrate Christmas, Easter, and the feast days of saints as well.

Except for national holidays and Christian festivals, other Vietnamese festivals are celebrated according to the lunar calendar. These festivals include Than Minh and Trung Nguyen, both of which are dedicated to remembering the dead, and Tet Doan Ngu, the summer solstice.

Left: **Pilgrims pray at the altars of the Perfume Pagoda in Hanoi during Tet.**

Opposite: **Dancers in traditional finery and bearing lighted lotus flowers perform at the Imperial City in Hue.**

THE LUNAR CALENDAR

The lunar calendar is based on the number of days between new moons, so there are only 29 or 30 days to a month, or 355 days to a year. The lunar year has 12 months, but once every three years a 13th month is added to keep the years in line with solar years.

The lunar calendar completes a cycle called a *hoi* every 60 years. The *hoi* is divided into 12-year periods, with each year named after an animal in the Buddhist zodiac. Year one is the year of the rat. This is followed by the buffalo, tiger, cat, dragon, snake, horse, goat, monkey, rooster, dog, and last of all pig. It is easy for a Vietnamese to guess a person's age simply by asking which animal of the zodiac the person belongs to. Each animal is believed to personify certain characteristics. For instance, roosters are courageous but flamboyant, goats are good-natured, and rats are shrewd.

The *hoi* is also divided into sets of 10 years. Each set of 10 years belongs to one of five elements—wood, water, fire, metal, or earth—in a natural or civilized state, for example, earth could be virgin (natural) or cultivated. Each year of a *hoi* therefore has a dual identity, for instance, the year of the fire horse.

NEW YEAR—TET NGUYEN DAN

The most important festival is the Vietnamese New Year, or Tet Nguyen Dan, which celebrates the beginning of spring. Tet, as it is often called, falls sometime in January or February. The date is determined by the lunar calendar, the same calendar used by the Chinese. As Tet usually occurs between the harvesting of one rice crop and the sowing of the next, farmers take this chance to rest and celebrate.

Much preparation must be made before the end of the lunar year. The extended family makes arrangements to meet for celebrations. Overseas Vietnamese book flights ahead of time to ensure that they return in time to celebrate the event.

Houses are given a thorough spring cleaning and decorated with peach blossoms, chrysanthemums, and apricot flowers to symbolize the arrival of spring. Streets are decorated with colored lights and red and pink banners. Ancestors are not forgotten. Family altars and ancestral graves are swept

Tet is a joyous occasion that is celebrated by Vietnamese in the cities and provinces.

and cleaned. It is also important to repay debts and to mend broken relationships before the new year.

On New Year's Eve, Vietnamese families offer incense, fruit, and flowers to the spirits of their ancestors. When the family gathers for a special New Year's Eve dinner, ancestral spirits are invited to join the feast. Another offering is made to the kitchen god, who will soon depart on his annual journey to the emperor of heaven. Families are anxious to keep the kitchen god happy because he gives the emperor an annual report on the family. Traditionally, long strings of firecrackers were hung from bamboo poles and set off, signifying the start of the new year and helping to drive off evil spirits. However, the number of injuries caused by firecrackers prompted a government ban that took effect on January 1, 1995.

It is believed that the first visitor on New Year's Day brings either good or bad luck to the household. So rather than leaving it to chance, Vietnamese prefer to invite a respected person to be the first visitor to their home on that day. Children receive gifts or money wrapped in red paper. Sweet lotus seeds, winter melon strips, coconut, kumquats, and other preserved fruit are eaten. The most important food prepared for Tet is *banh chung* (bahn ch-uhng), a sticky rice dumpling filled with mashed mung beans and pork.

Firecrackers are used to add to the gaiety of the Tet festival. After the government's firecracker ban, however, Tet celebrations have become quieter.

THE ORIGIN OF *BANH CHUNG*

A Vietnamese legend relates how King Hung Vuong VI devised a method of selecting the best of his 22 sons to succeed him. He decided to send all his sons to the farthest corners of the world in search of recipes and foods that he had never tasted. The one who returned with the best dish would become the king.

All the princes but one set out on long journeys to distant places. The 16th prince, Lang Lieu, remained at home. He had no idea how to go about the task. One night, a genie appeared in a dream and said, "It is a law of nature that man cannot live without rice; it is man's chief food."

The genie then gave Lang Lieu two recipes—one for *banh chung* and the other for *banh giay* (bahn zai). The next day the prince set out to collect the ingredients and, with the help of his old nurse, prepared the two cakes.

On the appointed day, the 22 princes presented their dishes. King Hung Vuong tasted each in turn but was not impressed.

Lang Lieu's turn came. He presented two cakes, one white and "round as the sky," the other wrapped in leaves and "square as the earth."

The king tasted each cake and was delighted. He asked Lang Lieu where he found the delicious food. Lang Lieu explained how a genie had appeared with recipes for the rice cakes.

The king named Lang Lieu his successor. He also decided to name the cakes *banh chung* (square as the earth) and *banh giay* (round as the sky).

SPRING FESTIVAL

The Muong, Tay, Tai, and other hill peoples celebrate the Spring Festival with a drinking party. Wine made from fermented rice is prepared throughout the year and stored in large earthen jars. Young and old sit around the jars drinking rice wine, and singing and dancing. They celebrate Tet in the same way.

Many villages hold special events in connection with Tet. In Quang Ngai there are horse races, and Lieu Doi holds wrestling matches.

RESPECTING THE DEAD

Thanh Minh and Trung Nguyen are dedicated to remembering the dead. Thanh Minh falls on the fifth day of the third lunar month. Vietnamese visit the graves of their relatives and ancestors. They clean the graves and bring food, paper money, and flowers to offer to the souls of their ancestors.

Vietnamese believe that on Trung Nguyen, the 15th day of the seventh lunar month, the souls of the dead are released to wander on earth for a month. Therefore, offerings of joss sticks, incense, and food are made at graves and temples to comfort the spirits and appease their hunger. The most pitiable souls are those whose descendants have neglected the rituals of offering and worship.

Only burned-out joss sticks remain at a grave, for the food is consumed by the living after its ceremonial offering during Trung Nguyen.

TET DOAN NGU

The fifth day of the fifth lunar month marks the summer solstice, or midsummer. Unlike the Western midsummer, Vietnamese regard this as an unhealthy time of year. To ward off sickness and bad luck, they burn paper effigies as offerings to the god of death. They also buy amulets from the temple for protection against evil spirits. The people of Nha Trang bathe in the sea on this day in the belief that this will kill the worms in the body.

TRUNG THU

The Mid-Autumn festival falls on the 15th day of the eighth lunar month. Children celebrate the festival with lantern parades, and everybody eats mooncakes, a wheat, or rice-flour pastry with a sweet sesame or bean paste filling. In the evening, people enjoy the beauty of the full moon, which is largest and brightest at this time of the year.

PHONG SINH

This festival commemorates Buddha's birthday, enlightenment, and death. Birds and fish in captivity are set free by Buddhists to honor the occasion. In northern parts of Vietnam, trained doves are released in teams of 10, and a contest is held to judge their aerobatic skill.

A boy with a Buddha image in a temple.

LAC LONG QUAN

This festival is held from the first to the sixth day of the third lunar month at Binh Minh village, Ha Son Binh province. It is dedicated to Lac Long Quan, the legendary ancestor of the Vietnamese. Elders dress in traditional silk robes, and young women carrying altars laden with flowers and fruit form a street parade in Binh Minh village. The parade is accompanied by traditional music.

INCENSE CEREMONY

The incense ceremony is held at the citadel of Co Loa. This ceremony used to be part of the rites that every Vietnamese king was required to perform in order to adhere to Confucian precepts.

Ho Chi Minh City held its first National Day celebration on September 2, 1975.

HOLIDAYS

The most important national holidays are National Day, Liberation Day, and Labor Day. Vietnam's National Day, which falls on September 2, marks the anniversary of Ho Chi Minh's Declaration of Independence in 1945 as well as the anniversary of his death in 1969. Liberation Day and International Labor Day, which fall on April 30 and May 1 respectively, are usually celebrated together. Liberation Day marks the time when the Vietcong liberated Saigon in 1975. Parades are held in every city, and workers usually present special performances such as musicals or concerts to mark the occasion. Vietnamese also celebrate the founding of the Communist Party (February 3) and Ho Chi Minh's birthday (May 19).

FOOD

ALTHOUGH VIETNAMESE FOOD shares many common characteristics with the cuisines of Thailand, Laos, and Cambodia, especially in the use of chili peppers, herbs, and other spices, Vietnamese cooking is less spicy and its combination of flavors more subtle. Vietnam, especially its northern region, is also more heavily influenced by Chinese methods of cooking than its Indochinese neighbors.

A FAMILY MEAL

As in most of Southeast Asia, cooking ingredients are bought daily, fresh from the market, and meals often consist of rice with vegetables, fish, meat, or beancurd.

Nuoc cham (nw-UHK chum), a dip made by adding vinegar or lime juice, sugar, finely chopped garlic, and some minced chili pepper to fish sauce, is used to add extra flavor to almost any Vietnamese dish.

Food may be placed on a low table, but a rural family may sit on straw mats on the floor around a pot of rice and bowls of other foods placed on a large round tray. Knives are not used at meals, as meat and vegetables are usually already cut into bite-sized portions so that they are easily picked up with chopsticks. Rice is served in individual bowls, but all other food is placed in communal bowls, and diners serve themselves using their own chopsticks or serving spoons. Traditional etiquette requires family members to wait until the father (or in an extended family, the grandfather) is at the table before the meal begins.

popular snack

Opposite: **Vietnamese crepes filled with meat, bean sprouts, onions, and mushrooms are a popular snack.**

Below: **A spread of traditional Vietnamese food. The bowl of** *nuoc cham* **(fish sauce dip, front) is indispensable at any Vietnamese meal.**

Table manners are fairly simple. It is polite to take food and place it in the rice bowl before eating it and not to transfer it straight from the serving dish to the mouth. When not being used, chopsticks should rest on top of the rice bowl or by its side. It is also considered rude to place chopsticks upright, sticking into the food.

In times of hardship, many Vietnamese survived on rice alone, flavored with salt or a little fish sauce, sometimes supplemented with vegetables or sweet potatoes.

A Vietnamese boy carries vegetables from the market on his bicycle.

REGIONAL SPECIALITIES

Because of geographical and historical differences, northern, central, and southern Vietnam have each developed different regional cuisines. Northern cuisine reflects greater Chinese influence as is evident in the different thick soups, stir-fried dishes, and restrained use of chilies.

The central region uses the most chilies, which is not surprising as this spice was introduced to Vietnam by the Portuguese who stopped at ports such as Da Nang in central Vietnam before heading for China and Japan

RICE

Rice is consumed in a great many different ways—rice flour is made into flat or round noodles, sweet and savory rice cakes, and translucent sheets of rice paper for wrapping the filling that goes into Vietnamese spring rolls. It is fermented in shrimp and fish pastes and fermented and distilled into rice wines. Sticky or glutinous rice known as *nep* (nep) is used in *banh chung* and in sweet soups known as *che* (chair).

in the 18th and 19th centuries.

The south shows the influence of Indian and Indonesian spices, again a result of trading activities beginning in the first century. In the 19th century, the French introduced tomatoes, potatoes, strawberries, coffee, ice cream, paté, and French bread. These have since become standard fare at Vietnam's numerous sidewalk cafés. Many towns and cities have their own specialities, some more exotic than others.

HANOI The northern city of Hanoi is famous for its thick soups—essentially a chicken or pork broth cooked with fish, eel, or crab, and slices of Chinese mushroom, wood ear fungus, and egg. A hot bowl of one of these soups is a fine way to start a meal, especially during the cooler months of the year. Visitors to Hanoi often look forward to a meal of *cha ca la vang* (CHAH kah lah VAHNG). Grilled chunks of catfish are served in a sizzling pan of fat kept hot over a charcoal fire. The fish is eaten with mint and coriander leaves, spring onions, peanuts, chilies, and fish sauce.

Vegetables are often eaten raw. Noodle soup stalls are found everywhere in Vietnam.

Noodle soup (stalls x ∽p)

HUE AND THE COAST Formerly the capital of the Nguyen dynasty, Hue offers a wide variety of fried or steamed rice cakes seasoned with minced meat, shrimp, and egg. Hue also boasts a noodle soup garnished with shrimp and meat that is much spicier than the *pho* (fuh), or noodle soups, in the north or south. The coastal cities of Da Nang and Nha Trang specialize in seafood—lobsters, prawns, fish, and crabs—while in nearby Phan Rang the speciality is baked gecko.

THE MEKONG DELTA People living in this region enjoy fish, eel, snake, turtle, and frog. These are sometimes served in a hot pot—a circular pan resembling an angel cake tin—that holds the meat and soup while a charcoal fire in the middle of the ring-like pan keeps the dish simmering throughout the meal.

POPULAR DISHES

Certain dishes are very popular throughout the country and may also be found on the menus of Vietnamese restaurants around the world. Of these, perhaps Vietnamese spring rolls and beef noodle soup are the best known.

Spring rolls are known as *cha gio* (chah geeo) in the south and *nem* (nem) in the north. Some restaurants offer two varieties—Hue style and Saigon style. The Hue spring roll has a meatier filling than the Saigon roll. Spring rolls are often served as appetizers before the main dishes are brought to the table. The rolls are made with thin, crispy rice paper filled with minced pork, crab, thin noodles, onion, mushroom, and a wafer-like, ear-shaped wood fungus known as *moc nhi* (moak nyee). They are served with lettuce leaves.

Other popular dishes are *banh cuon* (BAHN kwuhn), a steamed rice pancake filled with minced pork and dried shrimp and garnished with fried shallots, and *cha tom*, sticks of young sugarcane wrapped with ground shrimp and grilled. Beef noodle soup, or *pho bo* (fuh bo), and other noodle soups are very popular and make a satisfying one-dish meal. Flat rice noodles are garnished with slices of beef and served in a bowl of tasty broth. Noodle sellers usually provide customers with another large bowl that contains lettuce leaves, mint, basil, coriander, and other herbs to go with the noodles. Fish sauce and sliced chilies are the usual accompaniments, with a dash of lemon or lime for the soup.

Vietnamese women indulge in informal street dining where prices are affordable.

EATING OUT

In terms of cuisine, Ho Chi Minh City is the most cosmopolitan city in Vietnam. Apart from restaurants serving Vietnamese food, there are numerous eateries serving Chinese, French, and Italian meals. Recently, Japanese and Korean restaurants have opened in the upmarket business district. But most Vietnamese prefer to patronize one of the smaller cafés, family restaurants, or street stalls that offer an infinite variety of dishes at far more economical prices.

STREET STALLS Dining in the streets is very common in Vietnam. Food vendors selling *pho*, French bread with paté, shellfish, fertilized duck eggs, sweet soups, and desserts gather at street corners or line the alleys off a main street. Cooking is done over portable charcoal or firewood stoves, and patrons sit on tiny stools or low benches placed at tables no higher than the knee.

Many street stalls and family restaurants specialize in *com trang* (comb chang), which means high-quality rice. Stalls with this sign serve a wide variety of ready-cooked dishes to go with plain rice. A typical *com trang* stall may offer fried fish, braised vegetables, beancurd, pig's intestines, fish soup, pork slices, and salted egg, among other dishes. After the meal, bananas may be offered as dessert. Not too far off, one is likely to find vendors selling *che* (chay), a sweet soup made from coconut milk, to which lotus seeds, sliced bananas, boiled green beans, or sticky rice are added.

Sugarcane sellers at a market in Ho Chi Minh City. Sections of sugarcane are cleaned and run between the wheels of a mangler to make sugarcane juice, a refreshing drink when cooled with ice.

POPULAR BEVERAGES

The Vietnamese have a most refreshing antidote for humid, sultry afternoons in the form of *soda chanh*—a glass of crushed ice, lemon juice, and sugar topped with soda water. Coconut water and sugarcane juice are two other popular thirst quenchers, while *cuong thom*, a bitter, dark green drink made from crushed leaves, is said to cool the body.

Green tea, which is often served with a meal, is also sold hot or cold at roadside cafés. The drink to

PREPARING *NUOC MAM*

Nuoc mam (nw-UHK mam), or fish sauce, is the most commonly used flavoring in Vietnam. The clear, light brown sauce is strongly flavored and fairly thick before it is mixed with chili and lime juice or vinegar to become *nuoc cham,* the fish sauce dip found at just about every Vietnamese meal. *Nuoc mam* is made by placing various small fish in a large earthen vat of salt water. A stone is placed over the heap of fish to act as a press, and the fish are left to ferment for a few months before *nuoc mam* is obtained.

BIRD'S NEST SOUP

The Vietnamese, like the Chinese, prize the edible nests of the sea swallow, or salangane. Sea swallows do not build nests out of twigs or moss. Instead, they produce a sticky secretion from their beaks that dries and hardens like glue, from which their nests are formed. These nests are collected from cliffsides and sold at a high price because they are believed to have medicinal value. They have to be cleaned of feathers and other impurities, then soaked in water to soften them before being cooked in chicken broth to produce bird's nest soup. In Vietnam, the best quality nests are collected from the cliffs of Hon Yen (Salangane Island), near Nha Trang.

have at a café would be coffee, Vietnamese style, known as *ca phe sua* (with condensed milk) or *ca phe den* (black). In most places, *ca phe sua* is served in a glass with a metal coffee filter above it. Thick, dark coffee trickles slowly into the glass, which is already filled with a spoonful of sweetened condensed milk. When only the dregs are left in the filter, hot water from a flask is added to the milk and coffee, which is then stirred before it is drunk.

Vietnam produces its own beer, soft drinks, and mineral water, and these are becoming quite popular. Stalls are set up at resting points along highways where travelers can buy these drinks, pick up a sticky rice cake, or replenish their supply of cigarettes before proceeding to the next town.

Food is cooked on the spot and sold by vendors like this woman. Everything she needs is carried in two baskets, which are hung from a pole that goes over her shoulder. Charcoal stoves like the one in the picture are used in many homes.

COOKING EQUIPMENT

The Vietnamese kitchen is fairly simple. In rural areas, it may be a small outdoor shed attached to the house. Ovens are seldom found, and food is usually cooked over a clay or brick stove, using charcoal or firewood for fuel. Grilling, frying, boiling, and steaming are the usual cooking methods. Fish, meat, or rice may be grilled over charcoal, wrapped in banana leaves, or secured in a wire mesh. Most dishes require very little fat in their preparation, and tomatoes and pineapple are often added to soup.

Basic equipment needed in the kitchen are the *chao* (chow), a frying pan with a curved bottom that is called a wok in China, a cleaver, and a wooden chopping board. Meat and vegetables are cut into bite-sized portions for most dishes, and chili peppers and other condiments are reduced to a fine mince with the cleaver. To prepare dishes such as *banh cuon* and other pancakes, a griddle is necessary.

Few households possess a refrigerator, but this is not a necessity since Vietnamese buy fresh food daily from the market.

RECIPE FOR *PHO BO* (BEEF NOODLE SOUP)

This recipe serves eight.

Ingredients for stock:
1 pound (450 g) beef
1 large marrow bone
2 large onions, halved
1 star anise
2-inch (5 cm) piece of fresh ginger
6½ pints (3 liters) water

Other ingredients:
2 pounds (900 g) dried rice
  noodles
1 pound (450 g) rump steak
chopped shallots
mint leaves

Put all the stock ingredients in a large saucepan and boil.

Remove scum, cover the pan, and reduce the heat to low, leaving the stock to simmer for three hours. Pour the stock through a strainer and skim off the fat.

While the stock is simmering, fill another saucepan with water and boil. Add a pinch of salt and then the dried rice noodles. Boil for about five minutes. The noodles should not be overcooked. Drain in a colander and divide into eight deep soup bowls.

Cut the rump steak into very thin slices that are about 1 inch long (2.5 cm) and ¼ inch wide (1 cm), and put the meat over the noodles.

To serve, boil the strained stock and pour over the noodles. Serve with chopped shallots and mint leaves in a side dish. Also have some *nuoc cham* prepared for dipping.

RECIPE FOR *NUOC CHAM* (FISH SAUCE)

1 clove garlic
1 small red chili pepper
1 teaspoon sugar
2 tablespoons cold water
1 tablespoon rice or malt vinegar (or juice from half a lime)
3 tablespoons fish sauce

Crush the garlic with the side of a heavy knife, then mince the chili and garlic finely. Add sugar, water, and lime juice or vinegar to the fish sauce and mix. Add the minced chili and garlic. Serve in a deep saucer.

"Vietnam today is awakening to a new life. Much of the old grand cuisine remains dormant, waiting to be revived by the tourist dollar and astute entrepreneurs …"

—Carol Selvarajah, *The Best of Asian Seafood*

SEABASS WITH TOMATO SOUP

This recipe serves one.

$^1/_2$ medium-sized tomato, diced
1 cup water
2 tablespoons fish sauce
2 teaspoons lime juice
pinch of sugar
pinch of salt

1 onion, sliced
1 chili, sliced
$3^1/_2$ ounces (100 g) seabass, sliced into
    1-inch (2.5-cm) pieces
1 tablespoon spring onions, chopped

Stir-fry the tomatoes. Add water and boil for a while. Put in the fish sauce, lime juice, sugar, salt, onions, and chili. Simmer for a few minutes before adding the sliced seabass. Bring to a boil. Garnish with the spring onions. Serve immediately.

CHA GIO (VIETNAMESE SPRING ROLLS)

This recipe makes 80 small rolls.

2 ounces (57 g) thin rice noodles
2 tablespoons dried tree ear mushroom
1 pound (¹/₂ kg) chicken, minced
8 ounces (227 g) crab meat
4 ounces (113 g) shrimp, shelled and chopped

1 large onion, sliced
3 garlic cloves, finely chopped
pinch of pepper
20 sheets round, dried rice paper
4 eggs, beaten
2 cups oil

Soak the rice noodles and mushroom separately in warm water. Drain the noodles after 20 minutes and cut into 1-inch pieces. Drain the mushroom after 30 minutes and chop finely. Put the noodles, mushroom, chicken, crab meat, shrimp, onion, cloves, and pepper in a bowl. Mix thoroughly. Cut a round rice paper sheet into quarters. Place the cut rice paper onto a flat surface. Using a pastry brush, paint the beaten eggs over the entire surface of the rice paper. Wait for two minutes so that the egg has enough time to soften it. When the rice paper looks soft and transparent, put one teaspoon of the filling near the curved side. Fold the side over to envelop the filling and continue to roll. Repeat the same steps for the other sheets of rice paper.

Pour the oil into a large frying pan, and put in the spring rolls. Turn the heat to moderate. Fry for 20 to 30 minutes until the rolls turn golden brown.

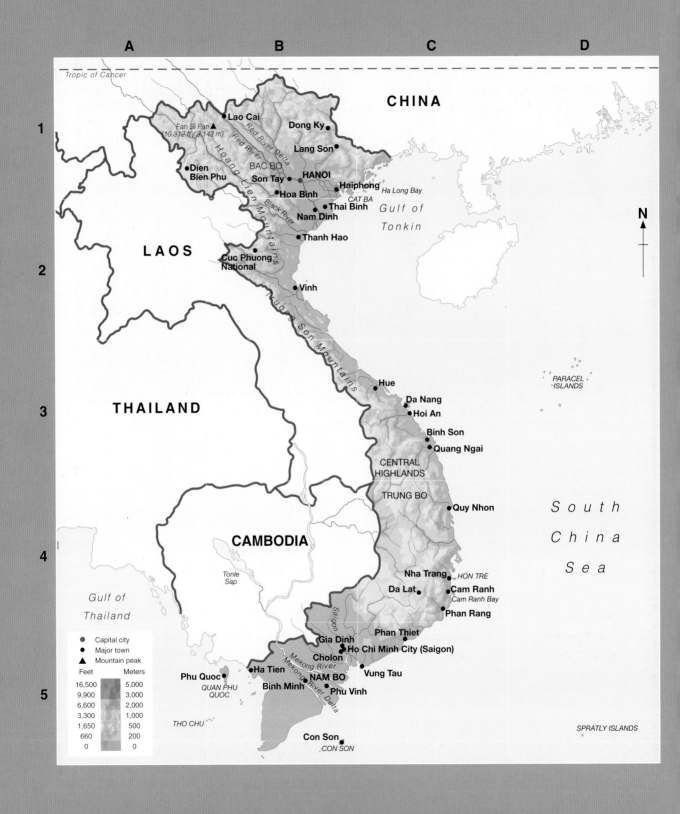

A **B** **C** **D**

Tropic of Cancer

CHINA

1
● Lao Cai
Fan Si Pan ▲
(10,312 ft / 3,142 m)
● Dong Ky
Red River Delta
● Lang Son
Red River
BAC BO
● Dien
Bien Phu
Son Tay ● ● HANOI
● Haiphong
Hoa Binh ● Ha Long Bay
CAT BA
Black River
● Thai Binh
Nam Dinh ●
Gulf of
Tonkin

LAOS

● Thanh Hao

Cuc Phuong
National
2
● Vinh

Truong Son Mountains
Hoang Lien Mountains

THAILAND

3
● Hue

PARACEL
ISLANDS
● Da Nang
● Hoi An

● Binh Son
● Quang Ngai

CENTRAL
HIGHLANDS

TRUNG BO
● Quy Nhon

S o u t h

C h i n a

CAMBODIA

Tonle
Sap

4
● Nha Trang *HON TRE*
● Da Lat
● Cam Ranh
Cam Ranh Bay
● Phan Rang

S e a

● Phan Thiet

Saigon
● Gia Dinh
● Ho Chi Minh City (Saigon)
Cholon

Gulf of
Thailand

Mekong River
● Ha Tien
NAM BO
● Vung Tau

● Phu Quoc
● Binh Minh
Mekong River Delta
● Phu Vinh

● Capital city
● Major town
▲ Mountain peak

QUAN PHU
QUOC

Feet   Meters
16,500   5,000
9,900   3,000
6,600   2,000
3,300   1,000
1,650   500
660   200
0   0

THO CHU

5
● Con Son
CON SON

SPRATLY ISLANDS

N
↑

MAP OF VIETNAM

ECONOMIC VIETNAM

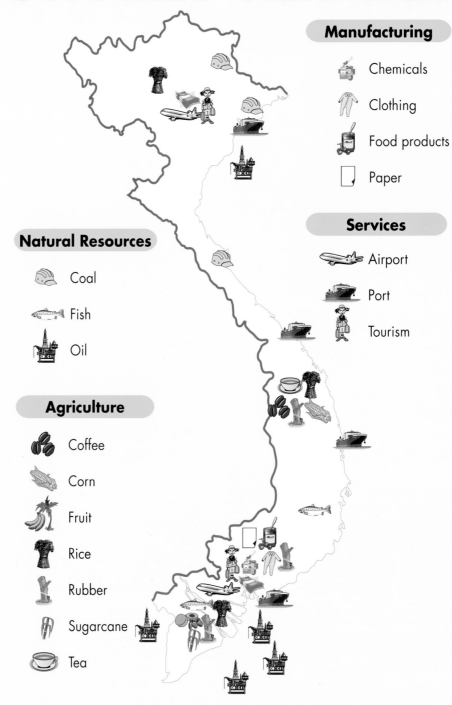

Manufacturing

- Chemicals
- Clothing
- Food products
- Paper

Services

- Airport
- Port
- Tourism

Natural Resources

- Coal
- Fish
- Oil

Agriculture

- Coffee
- Corn
- Fruit
- Rice
- Rubber
- Sugarcane
- Tea

ABOUT
THE ECONOMY

GROSS DOMESTIC PRODUCT (GDP)
$183 billion (2002)

GDP REAL GROWTH RATE
6 percent (2002)

GDP SECTORS
Services 39 percent, industry 37 percent, agriculture 24 percent (2001)

LAND AREA
127,211 square miles (329,560 square km)

LAND USE
Arable land 17.4 percent, permanent crops 4.7 percent, others 77.9 percent (1998)

AGRICULTURAL PRODUCTS
Rice, corn, potatoes, rubber, soybeans, coffee, tea, bananas, sugar, poultry, pork, fish

INDUSTRIAL PRODUCTS
Food products, clothing, footwear, machinery, cement, chemical fertilizer, glass, tires, oil, coal, steel, paper

CURRENCY
1 USD = 15,717 Vietnam dong (April 2004)
Notes: 100, 200, 500, 1,000, 2,000, 5,000, 10,000, 20,000, 50,000, 100,000 dong

LABOR FORCE
38.2 million (1998)

UNEMPLOYMENT RATE
25 percent (1995)

INFLATION RATE
3.9 percent (2002)

MAJOR TRADE PARTNERS
United States, Japan, Australia, China, Germany, Singapore, United Kingdom, South Korea, China, Japan, Singapore, Taiwan, Thailand

MAJOR EXPORTS
Crude oil, marine products, rice, coffee, tea, rubber, clothing, footwear

MAJOR IMPORTS
Machinery and equipment, petroleum products, fertilizer, steel products, raw cotton, grain, cement, motorcycles.

PORTS AND HARBORS
Cam Ranh, Da Nang, Haiphong, Ho Chi Minh City, Ha Long, Quy Nhon, Nha Trang, Vinh, Vung Tau

INTERNATIONAL PARTICIPATION
Association of Southeast Asian Nations (ASEAN); International Monetary Fund (IMF); International Criminal Police Organization (Interpol); International Organization for Standardization (ISO); United Nations (UN); United Nations Educational, Scientific, and Cultural Organization (UNESCO)

CULTURAL VIETNAM

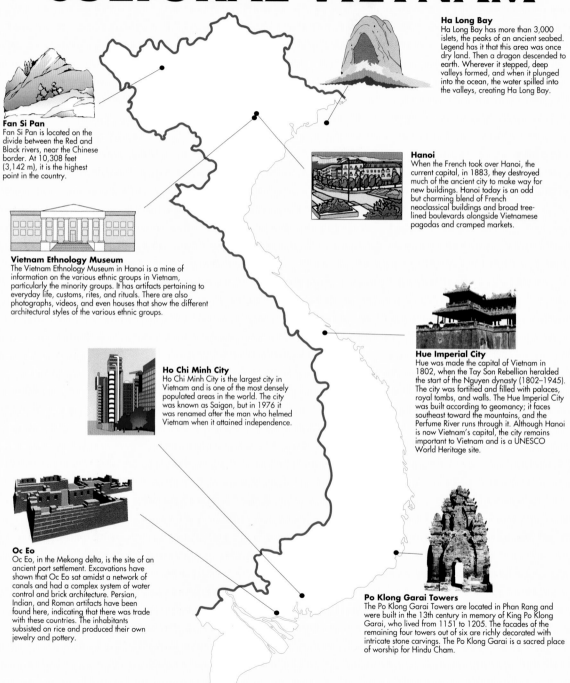

Ha Long Bay
Ha Long Bay has more than 3,000 islets, the peaks of an ancient seabed. Legend has it that this area was once dry land. Then a dragon descended to earth. Wherever it stepped, deep valleys formed, and when it plunged into the ocean, the water spilled into the valleys, creating Ha Long Bay.

Fan Si Pan
Fan Si Pan is located on the divide between the Red and Black rivers, near the Chinese border. At 10,308 feet (3,142 m), it is the highest point in the country.

Hanoi
When the French took over Hanoi, the current capital, in 1883, they destroyed much of the ancient city to make way for new buildings. Hanoi today is an odd but charming blend of French neoclassical buildings and broad tree-lined boulevards alongside Vietnamese pagodas and cramped markets.

Vietnam Ethnology Museum
The Vietnam Ethnology Museum in Hanoi is a mine of information on the various ethnic groups in Vietnam, particularly the minority groups. It has artifacts pertaining to everyday life, customs, rites, and rituals. There are also photographs, videos, and even houses that show the different architectural styles of the various ethnic groups.

Hue Imperial City
Hue was made the capital of Vietnam in 1802, when the Tay Son Rebellion heralded the start of the Nguyen dynasty (1802–1945). The city was fortified and filled with palaces, royal tombs, and walls. The Hue Imperial City was built according to geomancy; it faces southeast toward the mountains, and the Perfume River runs through it. Although Hanoi is now Vietnam's capital, the city remains important to Vietnam and is a UNESCO World Heritage site.

Ho Chi Minh City
Ho Chi Minh City is the largest city in Vietnam and is one of the most densely populated areas in the world. The city was known as Saigon, but in 1976 it was renamed after the man who helmed Vietnam when it attained independence.

Oc Eo
Oc Eo, in the Mekong delta, is the site of an ancient port settlement. Excavations have shown that Oc Eo sat amidst a network of canals and had a complex system of water control and brick architecture. Persian, Indian, and Roman artifacts have been found here, indicating that there was trade with these countries. The inhabitants subsisted on rice and produced their own jewelry and pottery.

Po Klong Garai Towers
The Po Klong Garai Towers are located in Phan Rang and were built in the 13th century in memory of King Po Klong Garai, who lived from 1151 to 1205. The facades of the remaining four towers out of six are richly decorated with intricate stone carvings. The Po Klong Garai is a sacred place of worship for Hindu Cham.

ABOUT THE CULTURE

OFFICIAL NAME
Socialist Republic of Vietnam

CAPITAL
Hanoi

OTHER MAJOR CITIES
Ho Chi Minh City, Danang, Haiphong

NATIONAL ANTHEM
Doan Quan Vietnam Di (March to the Front).
Adopted as the national anthem in 1976, the song
was written and composed by Van Cao (1923–95),
a musician, poet, and painter.

POPULATION
81,624,716 (July 2003)

POPULATION GROWTH RATE
1.3 percent (003)

LIFE EXPECTANCY
Men 67.6 years, women 72.7 years (2003)

ETHNIC GROUPS
Vietnamese 90 percent; Chinese, Hmong, Thai,
Khmer, Cham, mountain groups 10 percent

RELIGIONS
Buddhism, Hoa Hao, Cao Dai, Roman Catholicism,
Christianity, Islam, indigenous beliefs

LANGUAGES
Vietnamese (official); English, French, Chinese,
Khmer, mountain area languages (Mon-Khmer
and Malayo-Polynesian)

LITERACY RATE
94 percent (2003)

MAJOR HOLIDAYS
Vietnamese New Year (varies according to the
lunar calendar); Founding Day of the Communist
Party of Vietnam (February 3); Liberation Day of
South Vietnam and Saigon (April 30); International
Labor Day (May 1); Ho Chi Minh's birthday (May
19); Independence Day (September 2)

LEADERS IN POLITICS
Ho Chi Minh—president (1945–69)
Le Duc Anh—president (1992–97)
Tran Duc Luong—president since 1997
Phan Van Khai—prime minister since 1997
Nong Duc Manh—general secretary of the Vietnam
Communist Party since 2001; chairman of the
National Assembly (1992–2001)

FAMOUS VIETNAMESE
Nguyen Van Ty (painter), Le Thanh Nhon (sculptor),
Vu Trong Phung (writer), Doan Thi Diem (writer),
Nguyen Trai (scholar and poet).

TIME LINE

IN VIETNAM	IN THE WORLD
	753 B.C. Rome is founded.
	116–17 B.C. The Roman Empire reaches its greatest extent, under Emperor Trajan (98–17).
111 B.C. Chinese takeover of northern Vietnam	**A.D. 600** Height of Mayan civilization
A.D. 939 Ngo Quyen defeats Chinese armies at Bach Dang River.	**1000** The Chinese perfect gunpowder and begin to use it in warfare.
	1530 Beginning of trans-Atlantic slave trade organized by the Portuguese in Africa
	1558–1603 Reign of Elizabeth I of England
	1620 Pilgrims sail the *Mayflower* to America.
	1776 U.S. Declaration of Independence
	1789–99 The French Revolution
1859 French forces seize Saigon.	**1861** The U.S. Civil War begins.
1867 France colonizes Cochinchina.	**1869** The Suez Canal is opened.
1883 Vietnam falls fully under French rule, with Tonkin and Annam as protectorates.	**1914** World War I begins.
1940 Japanese troops occupy Indochina but allow the French to stay in their colony.	**1939** World War II begins.
1944–45 2 million North Vietnamese die from famine.	
1945 Japan surrenders. Ho Chi Minh reads the Vietnamese Declaration of Independence.	**1945** The United States drops atomic bombs on Hiroshima and Nagasaki.

IN VIETNAM	IN THE WORLD

1946
First Indochina War begins.

1949
The North Atlantic Treaty Organization (NATO) is formed.

1954
First Indochina war ends.
Vietnam is divided into North and South,
French forces to stay only in the South.

1955
Ngo Dinh Diem declares himself president of
the Republic of Vietnam.

1956
Second Indochina War begins.

1957
The Russians launch Sputnik.

1963
President Diem is assassinated.

1964
The United States imposes a trade embargo on
the North.

1966–69
The Chinese Cultural Revolution

1968
The United States and Vietnam take part in the
Paris Peace Talks.

1969
Ho Chi Minh dies.

1973
The United States and Vietnam sign the Paris
Peace Accords. U.S. troops leave Vietnam.

1975
Saigon falls. The United States imposes a trade
embargo on Vietnam.

1986
Nuclear power disaster at Chernobyl in
Ukraine

1991
Break-up of the Soviet Union

1994
U.S. trade embargo lifted

1997
Hong Kong is returned to China.

2000
Signing of trade agreement grants Vietnam the
same terms as most other countries.

2001
Terrorists crash planes in New York,
Washington, D.C., and Pennsylvania.

2003
Vietnam hosts the SEA Games.

2003
War in Iraq

GLOSSARY

ao-dai (ow-ZAI/ow-YAI)
The traditional dress for Vietnamese women.

ao the (ow-TUH)
Traditional men's clothing—a loose tunic worn over black or white pants.

ba (bah)
A term of respect used when addressing an older woman in Vietnam.

chu nho (chur nyawh)
Chinese ideographic characters used by the imperial court before the 13th century.

chu nom (chur noam)
The Vietnamese writing system based on Chinese characters; modified form of *chu nho*.

corvée (korh-VAY)
A system of forced labor under French rule.

doi moi (doy moy)
A term to describe the Vietnamese government's new economic policy.

em (em)
A form of address used between friends, relatives, and to younger persons.

guoc (gwok)
High-heeled wooden sandals worn with the traditional *ao dai* outfit.

hat tuong (hut tw-uhng)
Traditional theater with conventional dress and make-up so the characters are easy to identify.

khen (khen)
A mouth organ made from reeds.

kich noi (kik NOY)
Spoken drama.

non la (non lah)
A conical hat woven from palm leaves.

nuoc cham (nw-UHK chum)
Fish sauce used to accompany Vietnamese meals.

ong (awng)
A term of respect used when addressing an older man in Vietnam.

quoc ngu (kwok noo)
Romanized Vietnamese script.

roi nuoc (zoi nw-UHK)
Water puppetry, believed to have been developed in the 10th century.

Tet
The Vietnamese New Year, also known as Tet Nguyen Dan, which follows the lunar calendar.

to rung (toe RUHNG)
A bamboo xylophone.

FURTHER INFORMATION

BOOKS

Ashabranner, Brent. *Their Names to Live By*. Washington, D.C.: 21st Century Books, 1998.

Dunn, John M. *A History of U.S. Involvement: The Vietnam War*. San Diego, California: Lucent Books, 2000.

Garland, Shirley and Trina Schart Hyman (illustrator). *Children of the Dragon: Selected Tales from Vietnam*. San Diego, California: Harcourt Children's Books, 2001.

Kent, Deborah. *The Vietnam War: What Are We Fighting For?* American War Series. Berkeley Heights, New Jersey: Enslow Publishers, Inc., 2000.

Rice, Earle Jr. *Point of No Return: Tonkin Gulf and the Vietnam War*. First Battles. Greensboro, North Carolina: Morgan Reynolds, 2003.

Shalant, Phyllis. *Look What We've Brought You from Vietnam: Crafts, Games, Recipes, Stories, and Other Cultural Activities from Vietnamese Americans*. New York: Julian Messner, 1998.

Simpson, Judith and Valerie Hill (editor). *Vietnam*. Ask About Asia . Broomall, Pennsylvania: Mason Crest Publishers, 2003.

Steele, Philip. *Ho Chi Minh*. Leading Lives. Chicago, Illinois: Heinemann Library, 2003.

Townsend, Sue and Caroline Young. *Vietnam*. A World of Recipes. Chicago, Illinois: Heinemann Library, 2003.

Willis, Terry. *Vietnam*. Dublin, Ireland: Children's Press, 2002.

WEBSITES

Central Intelligence Agency World Factbook. www.cia.gov/cia/publications/factbook/geos/vm.html

Chronology of U.S.-Vietnam relations. http://servercc.oakton.edu/~wittman/chronol.htm

Ecology Asia. www.ecologyasia.com/index.htm

Embassy of Vietnam in the United States. www.vietnamembassy-usa.org/learn

Law on Water Resources. www.dk-vn.dk/dev_water_sanitation/LWR.htm

Online edition of Viet Nam News, the National English Language Daily newspaper.
    http://vietnamnews.vnagency.com.vn

Resource Centre on Urban Agriculture & Forestry. www.ruaf.org/reader/posters/hcmc.pdf

U.S. Embassy in Hanoi. http://hanoi.usembassy.gov

Vietnam Cleaner Production Centre. www.un.org.vn/vncpc/cp/iso.htm

World Health Organization Country Health Profiles. www.wpro.who.int/chip/vtn.htm

VIDEOS

Dear America—Letters Home from Vietnam. New York: HBO Studios, 1988.

Vietnam: Roots of War/First Vie. Boston: WGBH Boston Video, 1997.

BIBLIOGRAPHY

bibliography =

Cima, Ronald J. *Vietnam: A Country Study.* Washington, D.C.: U.S. Government Printing Office, 1994.

Cole, Wendy M. *Vietnam.* New York: Chelsea House, 1989.

Garland, Sherry. *Vietnam: Rebuilding a Nation.* New York: Macmillan Children's Book Group, 1990.

Nhuong, Nuynh Quang. *The Land I Lost: Adventures of a Boy in Vietnam.* New York: Harper Collins Children's Books, 1990.

Nickelson, Harry. *Vietnam.* San Diego, California: Lucent Books, 1989.

Vinh, Pham Kim. *Vietnamese Culture: An Introduction.* Revised edition. Fountain Valley, California: Pham Kim Vinh Research Institute, 1994.

Wright, David K. *Vietnam.* Chicago: Children's Press, 1989.

Vietnam—in Pictures. Minneapolis, Minnesota: Lerner Publications, 1994.

INDEX